T0091878

KIDNAPPING AND ABDUCTION

Minimizing the Threat and Lessons in Survival

KIDNAPPING AND ABDUCTION

Minimizing the Threat and Lessons in Survival

Brian John Heard

CRC Press
Taylor & Francis Group
Boca Raton London New York

CRC Press is an imprint of the
Taylor & Francis Group, an **informa** business

CRC Press
Taylor & Francis Group
6000 Broken Sound Parkway NW, Suite 300
Boca Raton, FL 33487-2742

© 2015 by Taylor & Francis Group, LLC
CRC Press is an imprint of Taylor & Francis Group, an Informa business

No claim to original U.S. Government works

Printed on acid-free paper
Version Date: 20140821

International Standard Book Number-13: 978-1-4822-2815-1 (Hardback)

This book contains information obtained from authentic and highly regarded sources. Reasonable efforts have been made to publish reliable data and information, but the author and publisher cannot assume responsibility for the validity of all materials or the consequences of their use. The authors and publishers have attempted to trace the copyright holders of all material reproduced in this publication and apologize to copyright holders if permission to publish in this form has not been obtained. If any copyright material has not been acknowledged please write and let us know so we may rectify in any future reprint.

Except as permitted under U.S. Copyright Law, no part of this book may be reprinted, reproduced, transmitted, or utilized in any form by any electronic, mechanical, or other means, now known or hereafter invented, including photocopying, microfilming, and recording, or in any information storage or retrieval system, without written permission from the publishers.

For permission to photocopy or use material electronically from this work, please access www.copyright.com (http://www.copyright.com/) or contact the Copyright Clearance Center, Inc. (CCC), 222 Rosewood Drive, Danvers, MA 01923, 978-750-8400. CCC is a not-for-profit organization that provides licenses and registration for a variety of users. For organizations that have been granted a photocopy license by the CCC, a separate system of payment has been arranged.

Trademark Notice: Product or corporate names may be trademarks or registered trademarks, and are used only for identification and explanation without intent to infringe.

Visit the Taylor & Francis Web site at
http://www.taylorandfrancis.com

and the CRC Press Web site at
http://www.crcpress.com

CONTENTS

1

Introduction

ABDUCTION OR KIDNAPPING, THE LEGAL DEFINITION

Originally, *kidnapping* was defined as the illegal capturing of a person with the intention of transporting him or her for slavery, and there was little differentiation between abduction and kidnapping. In the nineteenth century, the requirement for intercountry transport was eliminated.

Nowadays, *abduction* is legally defined as the process of capturing someone by force or fraud. Kidnapping also involves illegally detaining another person, but it does not have to involve fraud.

Kidnapping usually involves detaining another person with the intent to illegally detain him or her for ransom. Using the individual as a hostage for financial or some other reason is typically also involved. There are, however, several different characteristics separating abduction and kidnapping.

INTENT

Intent is not usually revealed in the case of abduction. For example, a sexual predator taking a child from school to molest him or her would be classified not as an abduction but rather as a kidnapping. However, the taking of a child for no reason is considered to be abduction. Abduction can be differentiated from kidnapping in that the public is made aware of the kidnapper's intentions, whereas those of the abductor are not certain. A kidnapper will always state the reason for the capture, whether it be for

1

ransom or some other reason. An abductor will often not state his* reason until after the victim has been found, regardless of whether the victim is dead or alive.

THE MONEY FACTOR

The abductor usually keeps the location and reason for the capture secret and typically will not involve the media. The kidnapper, on the other hand, will seek the media's influence to assist in obtaining his demands.

The abductor is generally seeking some gratification, whether this be through torture, murder, or something purely sexual, deviant, or otherwise, and is generally not seeking monetary or other rewards. The kidnapper, however, is interested only in some system of reward, whether this be monetary, the release of prisoners, or simply the dissemination of his or her political aims, and will, generally, keep the victim captive until the demands have been met.

Conversely, the abductor's reward is the act itself, and he will have no interest in anything other than that. Once the act of self-gratification has been satisfied, whatever that may be, the abduction is at an end.

VARYING LAWS

In some countries, legislation regarding abduction and kidnapping makes a distinction between the two. Kidnapping is, however, generally considered to involve the taking of a minor or adult by force, whereas abduction is viewed as being independent of age. In some countries, the legislation requires an element of deception to be involved before the crime can be classified as abduction.[1]

When considering kidnapping, most people initially think of those cases that have attracted considerable media coverage. Two such cases are the Lindbergh baby and the Patty Hearst kidnapping. It is also considered that kidnapping happens only to those with a high profile or who are very wealthy.

The majority of kidnappings go unreported, and as a result many consider kidnappings to be of minor importance. It is, however, far more

---

* For the sake of brevity and reader comprehension the masculine pronoun will be used when referring to the abductor/kidnapper.

prevalent than most suspect, with between 20,000 and 30,000 reported kidnappings each year.[2] Having said that, estimates are that up to 80 percent of such crimes go unreported, and the actual number of cases is certainly very much higher.

Kidnapping poses a serious risk for multinational companies, nongovernmental organizations, and the news media. Recognizing this risk, many large international corporations have developed strategies and policies to cover the security and safety of their staff and independent contractors. The recent availability of kidnap insurance, albeit at high cost, can cover the costs involved in kidnappings, as well as the employment of security consultants to respond to a kidnap situation. These insurance policies can also be structured to cover the costs involved in paying a ransom to have their staff released unharmed.

Kidnapping remains a relatively rare crime, but kidnappers are always evolving their strategies. This results in an ever-expanding requirement for multinationals to constantly review their knowledge and plans to thwart kidnappers.

At present there are six main types of kidnap cases, any of which can overlap:[3]

1. Express kidnapping
2. Tiger kidnapping
3. Political kidnapping
4. Kidnapping for ransom
5. Virtual kidnapping
6. Bride kidnapping

In *express kidnapping*, the victim is usually seized for not more than a couple of hours. This gives the kidnapper sufficient time to take the victim to an ATM (see Figure 1.1). The victim will then be forced to withdraw cash until the card's limit is reached. As this type of crime eliminates the necessity for prolonged surveillance, it is of lower risk to the kidnapper. It also tends to be more spontaneous, involving less planning and preparation than other types of kidnapping. Although this type of kidnapping can occur anywhere, it is most commonly encountered in Mexico, Colombia, Venezuela, Ecuador, and Brazil. It was also very common in Argentina following the political and economic crisis of 2001, but as of late it has become less so.

In some parts of South America, express kidnappings are also known as the *millionaire tour* or *millionaire walk*. In these cases, a taxi driver temporarily kidnaps an innocent passenger. The taxi then makes an unscheduled

Figure 1.1   In express kidnapping, the victim will be taken to an ATM and forced to withdraw cash.

stop to pick up an armed criminal who then forces the passenger to a variety of ATMs, withdrawing cash as before. The victim can then be further humiliated by being taken to his or her own house for the purposes of being further deprived of any items of value. Eventually, he or she will be drugged, often with scopolamine or ketamine, and abandoned in some remote location.

The second type of kidnapping is generally called *tiger kidnapping*. It is a type of kidnapping that was very commonly used by the Irish Republican Army and other terrorist organizations during the troubles in Northern Ireland. This type of kidnapping first involves the abduction of a close relation of the targeted individual. The targeted individual is then forced to carry out some illegal act in order to secure the release of his or her relation, who is usually a spouse, parent, or child. Normally, the illegal act would involve planting a bomb, undermining security barriers, opening a bank vault, or committing some other type of crime.

Tiger kidnappings are, since the cessation of the troubles in Northern Ireland, rare and tend to be carried out by someone remote from the criminal or terrorist organization. The predatory stalking that is required for this type of kidnapping gives the name of tiger kidnapping to this type of crime.

While the term *tiger kidnapping* was not in general use until the 1980s, the first recorded crime that can be described as such occurred in 1972.

After the 1980s, the crime became more widespread, and it became accepted as a type of kidnapping. The actual number of tiger kidnappings is very difficult to ascertain, as technically two crimes are committed, each of which can be used to generate a crime statistic. An added difficulty in compiling statistics for this type of kidnapping is that few are reported to police.[4] Tiger kidnappings are still quite widespread, but they are encountered more frequently in the United Kingdom, Ireland, and Belgium.

The third type of kidnapping is called *political kidnapping*. Political kidnapping does not usually involve holding the hostage for ransom but rather is utilized in an attempt to force a specific government to carry out the kidnappers' demands. These demands could include the release of prisoners, the withdrawal of troops, or even a change in governmental policy. Generally the kidnappers do not expect their demands to be met but rather envisage the garnering of press coverage for their cause and the release of political statements. The Taliban, Al-Qaeda, and other radical terrorist and jihadist groups use political kidnapping as a way of furthering their cause through the media (see Figure 1.2). Once media interest in the kidnapping has been fully exploited or the ransom has been paid, the victim is invariably executed. To extract the last iota of media interest from the kidnapping, the terrorist and jihadist groups involved generally video their victim's execution for release to Al Jazeera or via some other Internet-based forum.

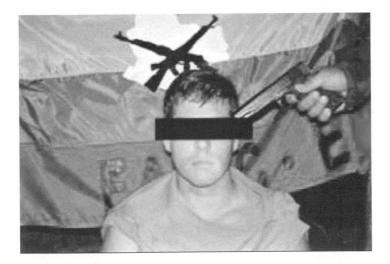

Figure 1.2 Hostage taking is an all too common terrorist tactic. (Photograph from Malcolm Nance, *Terrorist Recognition Handbook*, 3rd ed., CRC Press, 2014.)

Kidnapping for ransom is the fourth and most well-known type of kidnapping. This is a simple kidnapping scenario where the victim is abducted and a monetary demand is made for his or her release. Among crime statistics in general, it is not a common crime, but there are parts of the world where it is a real and constant threat. Although it is a simple exchange of victim for money crime, it does require considerably more planning and input of manpower than other types of kidnapping. There is also considerably more risk for the kidnapper, from being identified by the victim to the large number of opportunities for things to go wrong at all stages of the operation.

Virtual kidnapping is the fifth type of kidnapping, and it is more of a scam than that which is normally considered to be a kidnapping.[5] This type of kidnapping requires some research by the kidnappers, but only in respect of determining when the victim will be unreachable, for example, in a mobile phone dead area. The kidnappers will then contact the victim's family, demanding a small, but instant, ransom for his or her release. The victim is, of course, unaware that anything has happened and eventually returns home to discover that the family has paid a ransom for his or her "release." As the victim will probably be out of communication for only a short time, there is a need for speed, and as a result the ransoms demanded are nearly always very small.

A variation on this theme involves a call to the victim under the pretense that his or her mobile phone provider has a technical problem that requires the mobile phone to be turned off for a couple of hours. This achieves the same aim as waiting for the victim's phone to be out of signal coverage but is slightly easier to engineer.

As with express kidnappings, virtual kidnappings are most commonly encountered in Mexico, Colombia, Venezuela, Ecuador, and Brazil, although they can occur virtually anywhere.

Bride kidnapping, the last type of discernable kidnapping, does not really come within the purview of this book but is included for the sake of completion. Bride kidnapping is also known as *marriage by abduction* or *marriage by capture*. In this type of kidnapping, the victim is abducted, often by force, by a man who wishes to marry her.[6] Bride kidnapping is mainly restricted to the Caucasus region, Central Asia, the Romani in Europe, and certain areas of Africa. It is also prevalent among the Hmong tribes in China, Vietnam, Laos, and Thailand and the Tzeltal in Mexico.

Although some consider the practice to be a valid method of obtaining a bride, in most countries it is considered to be a sex crime. In Pakistan and India where arranged marriages are considered to be acceptable, there is a fine dividing line between bride kidnapping and a sex crime. Depending on the exact circumstances of the kidnapping, it may also be seen as falling somewhere between forced marriage and arranged marriage as practiced in India and Pakistan. Even in those countries where bride kidnapping is considered to be a crime, judicial enforcement often remains lax. Particularly noticeable in this respect are countries such as Turkey, Bulgaria, Kyrgyzstan, Moldova, and Chechnya.

While these examples give clear-cut examples of each type of kidnapping, there are those that cross over from one type to another. Terrorist and jihadist groups, for example, often conduct kidnappings for ransom to raise funds to further their political and religious aims. The revenue so obtained can be utilized to purchase weapons and generally fund their terrorist operations. The Taliban, for example, has done this quite extensively to easily raise large sums of money by ransoming victims.

Although kidnapping occurs throughout the world, the type and frequency of its incidence vary not only from country to country but also within certain countries. Afghanistan, Mexico, Brazil, Venezuela, Nigeria, Somalia, Chechnya, Iraq, Sudan, and Pakistan suffer to a great extent, as do many countries considered to be far more stable. For example, the United Kingdom, the United States, Hong Kong, Russia, and China, which one would not expect to have problems as far as this type of crime is concerned, do have their own kidnapping problems.

ENDNOTES

1. http://www.ehow.com/info_8591732_difference-between-abduction-kidnapping.html.
2. D. Concannon, *Kidnapping: An Investigator's Guide*, 2nd ed. (Elsevier, 2013).
3. www.threatrate.com/KIDNAPFORRANSOM/TypesofKidnappings.
4. www.thejournal.ie/five-year...rise-in-tiger-kidnappings-129220-Apr2011.
5. John L. Diamond, "Kidnapping: A Modern Definition," *American Journal of Criminal Law* 13 (1985): 1–36.
6. Frederic P. Miller, Agnes F. Vandome, and John McBrewster, *Bride Kidnapping* (Alphascript Publishing, 2010).

2

Demographic Distribution of Kidnap Incidents

The organizations and religious fanatics behind kidnapping incidents vary widely throughout the world, but for economic kidnapping to run as a money-generating process, it must operate through organized networks. These networks enable the group to operate over long distances, ease communication, and offer the stability that renders the breaking up of such groups difficult.

The groups, whether terrorist or jihadist in nature, that are involved in kidnapping are not unique to those countries where it presents a significant problem but as a result of the potentially low risks and high rewards present the groups can, under certain conditions, mobilize and kidnap for money on a large scale.

Kidnapping is not just country specific but more generally regionally specific within a country. Latin America, for example, accounts for almost half of all the worldwide kidnappings, but Pakistan, Somalia, Nigeria, Iraq, and Afghanistan account for the majority of the rest. Not unsurprisingly, kidnapping also tends to be concentrated in particular areas within any given country. For example, the capitals, major cities, and coastal areas generally account for the major portion of incidents, whereas the interior accounts for very few.

LATIN AMERICA

Mexico is, at present, perhaps the most serious kidnapping hotspot, although in 2012 South Africa and Somalia topped the list.[1]

In Mexico, the threat of kidnapping is greatest in Mexico City (see Figure 2.1) and along the northern border states, in particular Hermosillo and Chihuahua. As a result, Mexico City is often quoted as being the world's kidnapping capital. Between 2005 and 2012, the number of kidnapping-for-ransom cases tripled.[2]

While there are in excess of 1,000 reported kidnapping incidents per year in Mexico, the number of kidnappings is undoubtedly very much greater. This is partly due to the lack of trust in, and corruption within, the police and other law enforcement authorities. It has often been stated that in excess of 20 percent of the kidnappings in Mexico are attributable to the police or military.[3] As a result, few such crimes are reported.

Venezuela

Venezuela is currently considered to be one of the most violent places in the world, if not the most violent, with 21,692 murders in 2012 and an

Figure 2.1 An aerial photograph of Mexico City, Mexico. More than 47 percent of Mexico's entire population of 107 million people live below the poverty line.

estimated 17,000 kidnaps between 2008 and 2009. Venezuela's capital, Caracas, is currently listed as Latin America's most dangerous city.[4] Despite concerted efforts by the government, kidnappings, as well as almost all other crimes, have continued to rise.

As in Mexico, the official figure in Venezuela of 583 kidnappings in 2012 is likely to be much lower than actual numbers, as police sources indicate that as many as 80 percent of kidnappings go unreported.[5]

As a result of police corruption and a lackadaisical attitude to the investigation of kidnapping crime, whether it be traditional, express, or virtual kidnapping, this is a growing industry in Venezuela. The gangs that specialize in such kidnappings operate freely and without fear of investigation and conviction as a result of the police's attitude not just to kidnapping but also to crime in general.

The NGO Venezuelan Violence Observatory claims that there were 9,000 to 16,000 kidnappings in 2012.[6] However, because only a small portion of the incidents is ever reported and because of the unreliability of the figures, the number could be very much higher! As an example, in Caracas alone there were an estimated 5 kidnaps a day in 2012, giving a total in excess of 1,820 per year. With the vast number of kidnaps going unreported because of police corruption, the actual total is unknown.

Colombia

Colombia, a former kidnapper's playground, has dramatically reduced the incidence of kidnapping, although it is still very high.[7] *Diplomat Magazine* offers a good summary, and recent statistics, of the dangers of kidnapping:

> 2010 saw the first year-on-year increase in kidnapping in Colombia for a decade. According to the anti-kidnapping NGO Pais Libre,[8] the number of kidnappings rose 32% in 2010, to 282, with notable increases in the provinces of Huila, Meta, Norte de Santander and Nariño. This trend looks set to continue … given that the 177 kidnappings in the first quarter [of 2012] constitute a 35% rise on the same period in 2010. Nevertheless, this is still far below the peak of almost 2,600 in 1999.[9]

Brazil

As with many of the countries in South America, there is a significant threat of kidnap in Brazil. This includes Rio de Janeiro, São Paulo, and Campina in particular.[10] Kidnapping for ransom, lightning kidnapping—also called express kidnapping (*sequestro relampago* in Portuguese)—and virtual kidnappings are all a significant threat in all major cities.[11] The victims can be chosen as a result of perceived wealth, that is, expensive jewelry, vehicle, or even clothing, or simply at random on the streets.

Argentina

Kidnappings in Argentina are mainly carried out by common criminals and small gangs.[12] Executives visiting the country are not singled out as particular targets, and anyone, even of small perceived wealth, can be abducted. The abductions are generally only of short duration, and the victims are released once the ransom, which is usually quite modest, has been paid.

There are, however, criminal gangs in Buenos Aires specializing in express kidnappings,[13] but most of these incidents have taken place in downtown districts not usually visited by executives. Most of these kidnappings have been targeted at locals, or occasionally travelers, rather than visiting executives because of the short turnaround time necessary for such crimes to be successful.

El Salvador

Kidnapping is a very common crime in El Salvador, and kidnappings are usually carried out by professional gangs specializing in this type of crime.[14] As with most Latin American countries, law and order and the investigation of crime is of low priority, with corruption being rife. Kidnappings often occur in tourist areas and on city and rural roads. Because of the high threat level, it is generally recommended that executives travel in a convoy of at least two vehicles with one mobile phone minimum per vehicle.

Ecuador

Ecuador is, in general, a problematic area in terms of personal safety.[15] The Colombian province of Putumayo (see Figure 2.2) borders northern Ecuador and Peru. It is the region's major drug production area and, as such, has become one of the main targets for the United States's drug eradication plan for coca plants. Putumayo has become a battleground between leftist FARC guerrillas (Revolutionary Armed Forces of Colombia [Fuerzas Armadas Revolucionarias de Colombia]), the right-wing paramilitary units, and regular Colombian military forces.

Figure 2.2   The Colombian province of Putumayo.

All this activity has spilled over into Putumayo, and the FARC guerrillas and paramilitary fighters are using this part of the Ecuadorian Amazon basin as a safe heaven. As a result of all the paramilitary and guerrilla forces in the area, kidnapping of Canadian oil workers and travelers visiting the area has developed into a large money-generating business.

Guatemala

As in Ecuador, the majority of kidnappings in Guatemala are attributed to professional kidnapping gangs.[16] These gangs target executives and travelers arriving at the airport and taking taxis to hotels in Guatemala

City. Executives should be aware of the high threat level and use professionally trained security drivers and ensure there is an adequate security plan in place, as the police and other security forces may be disinclined to assist.

Haiti

Professional kidnap gangs remain a persistent risk throughout Haiti,[17] and the capital Port-au-Prince is a particular high-risk area. The majority of the targets for kidnappers are Haitian executives, missionaries, aid workers, foreign visitors and businessmen, and children. Most victims are speedily released after payment of a large ransom payout. Having said that, there are incidents where the victims have disappeared and presumed to have been killed.

With the recent influx of UN peacekeepers, incident rates have significantly decreased to the low hundreds. This is a significant reduction in the 2006 figures when some 720 incidents were recorded. However, a significant threat still persists, with abduction rates second only to Venezuela.

ASIA

Latin America is the world's foremost area for kidnapping; however, other areas of Asia remain almost as dangerous. Kidnapping is particularly common in Afghanistan, as the Taliban and other associated terrorist groups will often ransom individuals to raise money for their terrorist operations. The market is, in fact, so lucrative that the Taliban purchases abductees from criminal gangs to ransom on![18]

Kidnapping is also a problem in Pakistan, where, according to the executive security consulting company IMG Consulting, "there were 474 cases of kidnapping for ransom in 2010 and 467 cases in 2011. Although most of the victims were of Pakistani origin, there were at least 7, probably more, foreigners kidnapped in Pakistan between July 2011 and January 2012. Although most of the kidnappings in the country involved native Pakistanis, there were at least 7 foreigners kidnapped in the country between July 2011 in January 2012."[19]

Such high levels of kidnapping are not the preserve of Afghanistan and Pakistan, with kidnapping being a serious problem in what are considered to be more stable Asian countries.

Kidnapping poses a significant threat in the Philippines,[20] and the crime remains a problem in India, China, and Indonesia. While there were almost 35,000 reported kidnappings in India in 2009, many of these were so-called bride kidnappings. Such kidnappings are more common in New Delhi, Mumbai, Behar, and the Assam region of India. As an example, Delhi itself experienced almost 3,000 kidnappings in 2010.

Kidnapping is also on the rise on the other side of India's northeastern border with China. Although foreigners are rarely victims in China, kidnapping for ransom has been increasing. This is, however, mainly restricted to wealthy upper-class Chinese, with ransom demands of millions of U.S. dollars being quite common.

Hong Kong is also experiencing its share of kidnapping, although, as in China, this tends to be almost exclusively limited to rich Chinese businessmen and their families. A kidnap case in Hong Kong that was investigated by the author involved the abduction of Teddy Wang (born Teddy Wang Teihuei) in 1983. To prove that the kidnappers had Teddy Wang, they cut off his ear, took a Polaroid photograph of the injury (see Figure 2.3), and sent the photograph with the ear attached to his wife. A ransom of HK$66 million was demanded, of which his wife, Nina Wang, paid HK$33 million. He was never returned and was pronounced legally dead in 1999. His abductors were eventually convicted by way of a new technique called *reverse phase comparison microscopy*, developed by the author, which matched the Polaroid photograph to a camera found in the possession of one of the suspects.

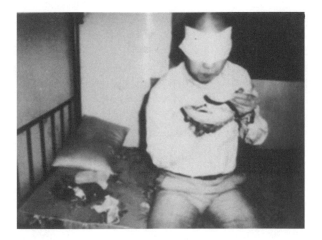

Figure 2.3   Polaroid photograph of kidnapped Hong Kong businessman.

15

The Philippines

Despite the image of the Philippines being a tropical paradise, there is a significant danger of kidnapping throughout the country.[21] This is particularly so in the southernmost part of Minanao, particularly Maguindanao, Lanao del Sur, Sulu, and Tawi-Tawi provinces. The whole area is part of the Autonomous Region in Muslim Mindanao (ARMM) and is home to a mainly Muslim population who are fighting for autonomy. These religious differences, exacerbated by rampant poverty, have led to the development of both an armed separatist movement and a communist insurgency. The areas of particular concern include dive sites and coastal and island tourist resorts. This is becoming a particular problem with live-aboard dive boats in remote locations such as the Sulu Sea.

The majority of kidnappings in the Philippines are attributed to extremist Muslim separatist groups, including ARMM. Kidnapping by common criminals is also a problem in the larger cities, with executives working or visiting these cities being favorite kidnap targets because of the ransoms paid for their release.

Kidnappers in the Philippines appear to be growing bolder, with the abductions of local upper-class citizens and local executives increasing in frequency. This is not, however, limited to executives, as the recent rescue by the Philippine National Police of a foreign couple who were kidnapped by gangsters as they walked out of Manila International Airport illustrates.

Westerners in the Philippines have also been kidnapped and robbed after being drugged by anesthetics with hallucinogenic properties. These are generally administered via drinks, food, chewing gum, or sweets.

According to the United States Overseas Security Advisory Council (OSAC): "Kidnapping for ransom" (KFR) remains a danger throughout the country. Several militant groups see KFR as way to fund their operations, and foreigners are often targeted. Philippine National Police statistics state that in 2011 there were 24 kidnap for ransom (KFR) cases throughout the country, down from 41 in 2010. In these 24 cases, there were a total of 38 victims. … Although kidnappings occur throughout the country, the majority of cases in 2011 were concentrated in Mindanao (Figure 2.4) and the Zamboanga Peninsula.[22]

Pakistan

In 2012, over 15,000 kidnappings were reported, although many of these were of the "bride kidnapping" type with no ransom demanded.

16

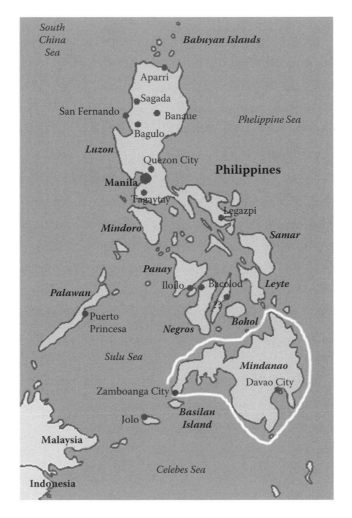

Figure 2.4 A map of the Philippines with Mindanao Island in ringed in white.

AFRICA

Africa also poses a significant and widespread threat of kidnapping, especially in places such as Algeria, Kenya, Nigeria, Somalia, Sudan, and the Democratic Republic of the Congo (DRC).[23] All suffer in particular from this type of crime, as well as those countries that compose and border the poorly patrolled Sahara Desert.[24]

The border region between Kenya and Somalia, as well as Nigeria and Benin, pose the largest threat areas for foreign nationals. The statistics for kidnaps in Africa are very poor, as most are carried out by locals against fellow citizens and go unreported. Many of these are simply a result of tribal disputes and would never come to the attention of the local police.

Algeria

The most recent danger to the region has been the threat posed by al-Qa'ida in the Islamic Maghreb (AQIM). Algerian forces have noted the group has run into financial struggles and shortages of personnel, and this has forced them to resort to kidnapping as a means of funding their operations. According to OSAC,

> Terrorist threats posed by al-Qa'ida in the Islamic Maghreb (AQIM) continue to dominate security concerns and media reporting. Regional instability brought about by revolutions in Tunisia, Egypt, and Libya along with a changing regional political climate has resulted in increased security concerns. ... Although AQIM's primary targets have been the government and its institutions, it has also targeted foreign interests. Kidnappings and the threat of kidnappings have prompted foreign governments and international organizations to warn their citizens, employees, and constituents against living, traveling, or working in the region.[25]

Sudan

Presently, violent crime, abduction, unmapped land mines, and general sociopolitical unrest make for a very unstable and dangerous environment in Sudan. Although there is considerable potential in the gas and oil industry, one should be very circumspect regarding travel in this most unstable of countries. There are few statistics available on kidnappings in the country, but OSAC reports,

> A steady increase in kidnap-for-profit incidents targeted foreigners working for INGOs and the UN in Darfur. While most of the kidnappings occurred during armed invasions of residences after dark, individuals have been targeted during the day, on the road, and in all three Darfur state capitals. More recently, a number of other foreign nationals have been abducted and held for ransom by criminal groups in Darfur. Armed militias are targeting South Sudan civilians in Khartoum. The threat of violent crime, including kidnappings,

armed robberies, home invasions, and carjackings is particularly high in Darfur, as the government has limited capacity to deter crime in that region.[26]

Somalia

Piracy in Somalia is well-known, with captured tankers and their crew being held for ransom and with the ships themselves generating sums in the millions of U.S. dollars.

While kidnapping individuals within the country occurs, Somalia is renowned for piracy and kidnapping on the high seas. In 2011, twenty-four vessels were reported seized with over 400 kidnappings off the coast of Somalia.

Any country transporting its crude oil off the coast of Somalia is at risk; however, Nigeria has been one of the biggest targets, losing almost 7 percent of its total crude oil revenue as a result of such criminality.[27]

As The Inkerman Group notes in its July 2012 proprietary publication *Kidnap and Ransom Monthly Review,*

> In perhaps a positive development for a continent plagued by piracy, Somali pirates released the crew of the Taiwanese Shiuh Fu No.1 vessel following eighteen months of captivity on 17 July 2012, after reportedly receiving a ransom payment of US$3 million. The release coincided with what appeared to be divisions within the pirates as well as their commanders, as reports later emerged that the pirates were being hunted by their local financiers. Although fractioning might be seen as a welcome development, as splits in piracy groups may hinder the ability of pirates to carry out successful operations, there is now a rising concern that the release could set off a series of violence clashes between rival pirate gangs and their various affiliates in the Hobyo district of Mudug, Somalia. Additionally, in a less-welcome report regarding the ongoing fight against international piracy, the UN monitoring group of Somalia detailed this month that there appears to be a "climate of impunity" enjoyed by pirate kingpins in Somalia, and added that one kingpin evaded capture after Somali President Sharif Ahmed awarded him a diplomatic passport.[28]

Gulf of Guinea

UN analysts, the United States, and others have now focused their attention on the Gulf of Guinea (see Figure 2.5), an area of increasing concern. The thought is that it is fast becoming the next piracy "hotspot."[29]

Figure 2.5 Note the Gulf of Guinea at the bottom of the map, a potential new hotbed for piracy.

While the piracy situation in the Gulf of Guinea is nothing like that seen off the coast of Somalia, it is feared that the pirates have spotted an area rich in commercial shipping but weak in maritime security. The coast is also extremely rough, offering numerous natural hideouts from which to mount attacks and to hide the ships and kidnapped seamen.

The Gulf of Guinea is now second in the world to Somalia in terms of piracy attacks and is already home to insurgency in the Niger Delta where the pirates routinely attack oil facilities. Some reports have gone so far as to estimate that piracy in the Gulf of Guinea has resulted in an estimated loss of $2 billion dollars annually.[30]

In April 2014, the U.S. Department of State issued a warning:

> U.S. citizens considering travel by sea near the Gulf of Guinea should exercise extreme caution, as there have been armed attacks, robberies, and kidnappings for ransom by pirates. There has ... been a recent rise in piracy and armed robbery in the Gulf of Guinea, including hijackings.

In addition, when transiting [in] the Gulf of Guinea, it is strongly recommended that vessels travel in convoys and maintain good communications at all times. U.S. citizens traveling on commercial passenger vessels should consult with the shipping or cruise ship company regarding precautions that will be taken to avoid hijacking incidents.[31]

Nigeria

There have, in the past few years, been several hundred kidnappings of expatriates on the Nigerian mainland, especially in the volatile area around the Niger Delta.[32] These kidnappings include tourists and gas and oil workers and executives. In 2012, there were over 1,000 kidnappings in the country as a whole. The Islamic terrorist group Boko Haram, from the remote northeast Boro state, is one of the numerous terrorist groups that are active in Nigeria. Another is the Lord's Resistance Army, a rebel Islamic group, which has been linked to kidnappings in Uganda, Sudan, and the DRC.

Democratic Republic of the Congo

Kidnappers in the DRC are, in the main, terrorists, criminal gangs, and undisciplined rank-and-file members of the army.[33] Their motivation is not simply political and religious but predominantly for financial gain and personal power. A particular problem for executives is being kidnapped by DRC soldiers at one of the numerous military roadblocks that occur throughout the country.

Zimbabwe

A political regime that is very aggressive to outsiders has made Zimbabwe more dangerous than ever for tourists and travelers.[34] Tourists and employees of foreign companies are considered to be opponents of the ruling political party. It is virtually impossible to travel safely anywhere in the country because of the lawlessness and state-sponsored violence against outsiders. In addition, the lack of infrastructure makes it almost impossible to do business on any sort of a firm footing. From 2011 to 2012, there were a reported 3,874 kidnappings, and from 2012 to 2013, there were a reported 4,333 kidnappings, an 11.8 percent change.

Algeria

Al-Qaeda in the Islamic Maghreb is one of the regional affiliates of Al-Qaeda in Algeria and is known to target expatriates for kidnapping.[35] However, Algerian security forces have observed that Al-Qaeda in the Islamic Maghreb has severe financial problems and a severe shortage of personnel. This has forced the terrorists into kidnapping fellow citizens for ransom as a way of generating money.

More here from its 2014 *Crime and Safety Report*:

> The U.S. Department of State rates Algeria as a Medium threat country for crime. … Military and police checkpoints are commonplace on major roads within large cities and throughout the countryside. Security personnel expect full cooperation. Drivers should maintain vigilance, as terrorists and criminals often employ false checkpoints as a tactic for ambushes and kidnappings, particularly in rural areas. This tactic is primarily used in the Kabylie regions of Boumerdes and Tizi Ouzou but is employed nationwide.
>
> Terrorist threats posed by al-Qa'ida in the Islamic Maghreb (AQIM) continue to dominate security concerns and media reporting. AQIM is the most active terrorist group in Algeria. … To increase its financial resources, AQIM has kidnapped Westerners in those countries to obtain ransoms.
>
> On January 16, 2013, "Those Who Sign in Blood," an AQIM-linked organization led by a former AQIM leader, Mokhtar Belmokhtar, attacked the Tiguentourine gas facility (a joint venture among Algerian, British, and Norwegian companies) near In Amenas, in southeastern Algeria. Over 800 people were taken hostage for several days, and the attack resulted in the deaths of 39 foreign hostages, including three U.S. citizens. The group's leader and an Algerian national, Mokhtar Belmokhtar, remains a threat and is at-large.[36]

THE MIDDLE EAST

Perhaps most visible, in terms of news coverage, are the latest kidnappings that have occurred in the Middle East. The now infamous ISIS (or often referred to as ISIL or the Islamic State) has captured and executed its victims on the world stage, seizing the attention of millions around the world and reminding us all of the very real threat of kidnap and violence that exists throughout the region.

Kidnapping is hardly a new tactic for terrorist groups in the Middle East—it has been employed by the many groups that predate or operate alongside ISIS. The hefty ransoms paid to release hostages and kidnapped persons from their detention have become a linchpin of terrorism funding.

In 2012, it was reported that Al-Qaeda, from which ISIS emerged, had reportedly earned roughly $120 million dollars in ransom money. In addition, reports surfaced in September 2014 that nearly £75 million had been paid to ISIS collectively over the five years prior. Western governments, conceding that this revenue stream has been vital in sustaining terrorist activity, have called on their fellow leaders to stop funding ISIS and other groups with the tens of millions of dollars that have been paid in ransom money thus far.

Israel

The majority of kidnappings in Israel are directed at Israeli soldiers and not tourists or company executives. For Israel this is becoming a serious problem, with thirty kidnap attempts between January 2013 and March 2013. In contrast there were only twenty-four kidnap attempts in 2012. The sole aim of these kidnappings is to trade Israel Defense Forces soldiers for the release of Palestinian prisoners.[37] Reports have stated that the kidnaps are, in the main, due to either Hamas or the Palestinian Islamic Jihad.

Yemen

There is a significant risk of kidnapping in Yemen, once again fueled by Al-Qaeda.[38] Unfortunately, the threat in the country is only likely to become exacerbated because of the recent political instability.[39]

The kidnappers are usually tribesmen who have grievances against the Yemeni government. They use the captives to demand the release of prisoners, the payment of a ransom, or, more usually, the execution of building projects in their areas. According to the *Yemen Times*, in an article in 2014, "An official source at the Yemeni Interior Ministry, who spoke to *Yemen Times* on condition of anonymity, said that over 14 incidents of kidnapping took place in 2012 and they all targeted foreigners, adding that the victims were released through tribal mediation."[40] Other figures report that 117 kidnappings took place in 2012, which only highlights the paucity of accurate figures in this region.

Iran

There is a considerable threat of kidnap in Iran, although the situation is somewhat different because of the anti-Western sentiment in the country.[41] The risk of kidnap by criminal or fanatical groups is low, but given the political tensions in the country, there is a significant risk that Iranian authorities could wrongfully detain Western travelers. Although this is not exactly kidnapping, it does qualify as being taken against one's will and held captive.

Afghanistan

Despite the West's intervention in the country, extremist and criminal groups in Afghanistan pose a serious kidnap threat to travelers and oil and gas personnel. As a result, the risk of being kidnapped and held hostage is high. Mines and booby traps along roads are often used as part of the abduction, and random stray gunshots pose an additional threat. When people are traveling by road, the use of end-to-end armed security support and hard-armored vehicles is a strongly recommended precaution.

The Taliban have carried out numerous kidnap attacks against foreign workers, NGOs, and private foreign companies. In 2012, there were an estimated 950 kidnappings in Afghanistan, although the true figure is undoubtedly very much higher.

THE UNITED STATES OF AMERICA

The United States has a high reported incidence of kidnapping, and there are certain states in which case numbers are unusually high.[42] For example, hundreds of cases of kidnapping occur in Phoenix, Arizona, with the majority being cross-border crimes perpetrated by human and drug syndicates from Mexico. The Phoenix Police Department has referred to the city as "the kidnapping capital in the United States" and, in a grant application to the Office of Justice Programs, note a total of 370 cases were reported in 2008. However, the U.S. Department of Justice inspector general "determined that only 59 of these incidents, or 34 percent, should have been classified as a kidnapping for crime reporting purposes."[43] So, the actual number of kidnaps is, therefore, somewhat open to discussion and, sometimes, heated debate.

During 1999, there were 203,900 children reported as the victims of family abductions in the United States and 58,200 of nonfamily abductions. Of these only 115 were, however, the results of unknown or of only slight acquaintance to the child.[44]

OTHER WESTERN COUNTRIES

Kidnapping is a concern in many other Western countries, including Greece, Spain, Georgia, Western Turkey, and the Caucasus region of Russia. As a result everyone traveling abroad, whether for business or pleasure, should, regardless of where they are traveling, be aware that the threat of kidnapping exists and should consult their foreign or overseas office for advice.

Kidnap Cases in the United Kingdom

Kidnap statistics for the United Kingdom are all but impossible to obtain because of the different ways in which each force records and handles such crimes. Those figures that are available relate mainly to those reported in London by the Metropolitan Police.

In the past couple of years, there has been a surge in extortion rackets organized by Eastern European gangs, which have substantially increased the number of kidnappings in the capital. The average for the capital is now running at about 365 kidnappings per year.

In London nearly 50 percent of all kidnappers and victims are foreign nationals,[45] usually from the same ethnic group. Much of this is attributable to the open border policies with the European Union, which has resulted in a huge increase in the numbers of foreign criminal networks in the largest cities and in particular London. The vicious gangs, mainly from Eastern Europe, that carry out these kidnappings have led to increasingly complex and high-risk situations, with each syndicate bringing its own criminal methodology and enterprises with it.

Although the Metropolitan Police report that in London there were a total of 358 kidnaps in 2010, the Met's specialist kidnap unit—the only one in the United Kingdom—worked on only 80 of those cases. In the other 300 or so cases, the police were notified only after a ransom was paid and the victim freed. The true figure for London is probably very much higher, as many such foreign-gang-based crimes go unreported.

With so many foreign nationals being involved in kidnaps, it often results in a requirement for the Metropolitan Police to work with police forces from several different countries. For example, a kidnap victim might be taken in London, but the ransom demand will be made in India.

In the United Kingdom generally and in the big cities in particular, kidnapping is particularly prevalent in the Chinese, South Asian, African, and Eastern European communities. These kidnappings generally involve torture and extreme violence, often with demands for only relatively small amounts of money.

According to the *Guardian* (UK),

> In one case a group of Lithuanian men seized a young Lithuanian after overhearing his accent in the pub. They beat him senseless and then

scrolled down the numbers in his mobile phone, calling friends and relatives to demand £200. Police rescued the critically injured victim, who spent weeks on a life support machine but eventually recovered.[46]

The perpetrators were never brought to justice.

The Metropolitan Police kidnap unit, which was established in 2001, has enjoyed a 100 percent success rate in recovering victims alive, but the prosecution rate has been very low because of the difficulties in getting witnesses to testify.[47]

Russia

In Russia, kidnappings are invariably carried out by organized terrorist and criminal gangs, with the motivation being primarily political but also for financial gain and increased personal power. The kidnappers are very sophisticated and do kidnap foreign tourists for ransom. Many Westerners have vanished in Chechnya and remain unaccounted for.

According to OSAC,

> Kidnappings frequently occur in the North Caucasus, mostly to obtain ransoms, although some are political in nature and have occasionally resulted in execution of the victims. Outside of the Caucus region, kidnappings occur with much less frequency and generally are not a problem.[48]

As stated earlier, it is extremely difficult to provide accurate or even approximate numbers for kidnap in Russia because of the small number that is reported and the corruption within the law-keeping agencies.

Chechnya

Chechnya is not by any stretch of the imagination a tourist destination, although expanding business opportunities in the gas and oil industry will result in executives with business interests visiting this country. Chechnya is an unstable, violent country that has been blighted by war and poverty for many. With unexploded mines, terrorist bombings, and kidnappings over much of the country, one has to be extremely circumspect about traveling there. One other slight problem with Chechnya in relation to business or personal visits concerns the complete lack of hotels in the country.

Statistics for any type of crime let alone kidnapping for Chechnya are all but impossible to obtain. Estimates indicate that there were 150 kidnappings in 2009, but since then very little additional information has been released. However, in October 2013, it was reported that the ICPO's Department for the Chechen Republic was running over 120 criminal cases of kidnapping, but this is suspected as being just the tip of the iceberg. Bride kidnapping is rife in the republic, but once again figures are very few and far between.

The following tables provide a summary of the previous discussion. Table 2.1 provides a short list of the kidnappings reported in 2012. Table 2.2 shows an example of how the crime of kidnapping changes from year to year. Table 2.3 presents the gangs and organizations involved in kidnapping.

Table 2.1 Number of Abductions Reported in the Year 2012

Country	Number
South Africa	3,874
Somalia	2,527
Mexico	1,642
Afghanistan	902
Pakistan	430
India	341
Colombia	285
Democratic Republic of the Congo	189
Sudan	159
Yemen	117
Central African Republic	115
Iraq	111
Gaza Strip	107
Philippines	102
Turkey	63
Burma	25
Nigeria	17

Note: The figures in this table were extracted from the references at the end of this chapter.

Table 2.2 Kidnapping Figures for Various Countries for the Years 1992–1999 and 2013

Country	1992	1994	1995	1997	1999	2012
Colombia	464	217	469	908	972	285
Mexico	46	31	48	275	402	1,642*
Former Soviet Union**	5	13	3	41	105	
Brazil	94	73	56	67	51	
Philippines	53	78	61	61	39	102
Nigeria	1	0	1	2	24	17
India	9	13	9	8	17	341
Ecuador	1	15	11	5	12	
Venezuela	15	7	7	24	12	2,915**
South Africa**	0	0	1	0	10	3,874

Note: The figures in this table were extracted from the references at the end of this chapter.
* As reported by Mexico's Federal Police. The nongovernmental organizations associated with the United Nations, however, place the number as high as 26,280.
** Estimated from government figures that are believed to represent only 20 percent of the actual kidnappings.

Table 2.3 The Gangs and Terrorist Groups Involved in Kidnapping

Country	Kidnapping Organizations
Colombia	Marxist-Leninist guerrillas FARC (Revolutionary Armed Forces of Colombia [Fuerzas Armadas Revolucionarias de Colombia]) ELN (National Liberation Army) EPL (Popular Liberation Army) Paramilitary groups Criminal (drugs) groups
Mexico	Criminal groups
Philippines	Criminal groups NPA (New People's Army) MILF (Moro Islamic Liberation Front) Abu Sayyaf (Islamic fundamentalists)
Ecuador	Criminal groups Ex-paramilitary fighters known as the Black Eagles
Venezuela	Criminal groups Red Flag (Bandera Roja), a former Marxist terrorist insurgent group United Self-Defense Forces of Venezuela (AUV) Shiite Hezbollah terrorist group (rumored)

Table 2.3 (*Continued*)   The Gangs and Terrorist Groups Involved in Kidnapping

Country	Kidnapping Organizations
Nigeria	Discontented villagers and youths Islamic terrorist group Boko Haram, from the remote northeast Boro state
Haiti	Coalition of National Brigades Hector Riobe Brigade Tontons Macoutes
India	Tamil Tigers (Sri Lankan group operating in India)
Former Soviet Union Russia	Criminal gangs Chechen rebels
Contemporary Russia	Seventeen terrorist groups, including those of the former USSR, have been banned by the Russian State including Al-Qaeda, the Taliban, The Muslim Brotherhood, Al-Jama'ah al-Islamiyyah, Usbat al-Ansar, Tanzim al-Jihad, Hizb al-Tahrir al-Islami, Lashkar-e Taiba, Jamaat-e Islami, Al-Hizb al-Islami fi Turkistan, Jam'iyyat al-Islah al-Ijtima'I, Jam'iyyat Ihya' al-Turath al-Islami, Mu'assasat al-Haramain, Majlis al-Shura al-Harbi al-A'la li-Quwwat al-Mujahedin fil-Shishan, Majlis Ishkiria wa-Daghestan, Jund al-Sham, Jama'at al-Mujahedin[49]
Uzbekistan	IMU (Islamic Movement of Uzbekistan)
Iraq	Tawhid and Jihad ("Oneness of God and Jihad") Islamic extremist group Insurgents, terrorists, and criminal groups The League of the Righteous
Bangladesh	Shanti Bahini rebel group United Peoples Democratic Front (UPDF), a terrorist group
Turkey	Kurdistan Worker's Party (PKK) Kurdish militants
Algeria	Al-Qaeda in the Islamic Maghreb (AQIM) Battalion of Blood group Khaled Abu al-Abbas Brigade
Hong Kong	Triads (WoHopTo, WoShingWo, Rung, Tung, Chuen, Shing, SunYeeOn, 14K, and Luen) and the mainland gangs such as the Daai Hunge Jai (Big Circle Gang)
China	Mainly the Daai Hunge Jai, but also various Triad groups Muslim Uyghur ethnic group, primarily in the northwestern province of Xinjiang

Note: The information in this table was extracted from the references at the end of this chapter.

KIDNAPPING BY TERRORISTS

As can be seen from Table 2.3, many groups, gangs, and individuals are involved in the business of kidnapping. Some are carried out by gangs of criminals, others occur purely for political purposes, and many are interfamily kidnappings where no money exchange is involved. The most serious, however, are those carried out by terrorists whose main objective is to obtain a ransom to fund purchase of their weaponry. Terrorist kidnappings often end up with the victims being killed not just because they have outlived their purpose but also for the media interest such killings bring to the terrorists' cause. This type of kidnapping is extremely serious. The threat of terrorism and the acts of violence associated with terrorism have never been greater.

Terrorist incidents of extortion and kidnap for ransom increased dramatically from 2007 to 2009. Recently, however, there has been a steady decline in numbers. That is not to say that one should be complacent when traveling or working abroad; in fact exactly the opposite is true. Executives, aid workers, doctors, and peacekeepers are now seen as a legitimate target by terrorists to finance their operations and purchase of weapons.

A table listing the terrorist groups operating in various countries that are or may be involved in kidnapping is provided in Appendix 1.

SOURCES

wikipedia.org/wiki/Foreign_hostages_in_Somalia.
www.forbes.com/.../china-kidnapping-guanxi-leadership-managing-hui.
www.bbc.co.uk/news/world-asia-china-24313452.
www.foxnews.com/.../welcome-to-venezuela-kidnap-capital-latin-americ.
www.nationmaster.com/graph/cri_kid-crime-kidnappings.
www.smartraveller.gov.au › Travel Bulletin.
"Crime in Venezuela: Shooting the Messenger," *The Economist*, August 18, 2010.
"Venezuela, More Deadly Than Iraq, Wonders Why," *New York Times*, August 22, 2010.
https://www.osac.gov/pages/ContentReportDetails.aspx?cid=13972.
colombiareports.co/colombia-kidnapping-statistics/.
http://www.mediosparalapaz.org/?idcategoria=46.
wikipedia.org/wiki/Crime_in_Haiti.
U.S. Department of State, "Haiti: Country-Specific Information" (November 23, 2009).
www.canada.com/Foreign+Affairs...kidnapped+Haiti.
Phil Sylvester, safety.worldnomads.com/Haiti/.../Haiti-High-Crime-and-Chaos.
Brazil Statistics and Data, www.ceicdata.com/.
"Óbitospor Causas Externas 1996 a 2010" (in Portuguese).

Alessandra Heinemann, *Crime and Violence in Development: A Literature Review of Latin America and the Caribbean* (World Bank, 2006).

Ferdinand von Schirach, *Crime and Guilt* (New York: Vintage, 2012).

"Brazil's Evolving Kidnap Culture," news.bbc.co.uk/2/hi/programs/this_world/4898554.stm.

www.nationmaster.com › South America › Brazil.

Asian crime statistics; www.mapsofworld.com › World Top Ten.

www.police.gov.hk › Home › Statistics.

wikipedia.org/wiki/Crime_in_Singapore.

"2013 Crime Stats for Pakistan," https://www.osac.gov/pages/ContentReport Details.aspx?cid=1375.

wikipedia.org/wiki/Crime_in_Pakistan.

Veena Kukreja, *Contemporary Pakistan: Political Processes, Conflicts, and Crises* (Sage, 2003), p. 193.

"CIA World Factbook-Pakistan," CIA World Factbook.

http://www.africacheck.org/reports/factsheet-south-africas-official-crime-statistics-for-201213/.

www.city-data.com/crime/crime-Sudan-Texas.html.

www.nationmaster.com › Africa › Sudan.

www.undp.org/...sudan/.../south-sudan-launches-crime-statistics-reports.

E. Benjamin Skinner, *A Crime So Monstrous: Face-to-Face with Modern-Day Slavery* (New York: Free Press, 2008).

somalilandpress.com/crime-rate-soars-in-somaliland-37410.

www.nationmaster.com › Africa › Somalia.

wikipedia.org/wiki/Foreign_hostages_in_Somalia.

www.economist.com/.../21586355-kidnapping-nigeria

"Chronology of Nigerian Militants' Attacks (Nigeria, Africa & World News)," Africamasterweb.com.

wikipedia.org/wiki/Foreign_hostages_in_Nigeria.

"Algerian Hostage Crisis," www.theguardian.com › News › World News.

Icon Group International, *Kidnappings: Webster's Facts and Phrases* (May 1, 2009).

"Kidnapping Risk High in the Dominican Republic of Congo," www.upi.com › Top News › Special Reports.

"Kidnapping in Zambia," knoema.com › World Data Atlas › Country Profiles › Zimbabwe.

www.meforum.org/793/how-to-deal-with-kidnappings-in-iraq.

wikipedia.org/wiki/Foreign_hostages_in_Afghanistan.

afpak.foreignpolicy.com/.../the_big_business_of_kidnapping_in_afghanistan.

"Express Kidnappings in Guatemala," travel.state.gov/travel/cis_pa_tw/cis/cis_1129.html.

wikipedia.org/wiki/Crime_in_Guatemala.

U.S. Department of State, "Guatemala: Country-Specific Information" (November 23, 2009).

www.fbi.gov/wanted/kidnap; USA.

www.nationmaster.com/graph/cri_kid-crime-kidnappings; USA.

http://wiki.answers.com/Q/How_many_people_are_kidnapped_each_day_in_
the_US.
"Countries Compared," www.nationmaster.com/graph/cri_kid-crime-kidnappings.
"Child Abduction in England and Wales: The Key Numbers," www.theguardian.
com › News › UK News › April Jones.
Mary Quin, *Kidnapped in Yemen: One Woman's Amazing Escape from Terrorist Captivity*
(Mainstream Publishing, 2006).

ENDNOTES

1. www.latinamericanstudies.org/mexico/kidnaps.htm.
2. http://www.havocscope.com/tag/kidnap-and-ransom/.
3. http://imgsecurity.net/kidnapping-part-ii-the-geography-of-the-crime/.
4. http://www.csmonitor.com/World/Americas/Latin-America-Monitor/
2012/0821/Caracas.
5. travel.state.gov/travel/cis_pa_tw/cis/cis_1059.htm.
6. https://www.osac.gov/Pages/ContentReportDetails.aspx?cid=13038.
7. imgsecurity.net/kidnapping-part-ii-the-geography-of-the-crime.
8. colombiareports.co/kidnappings-on-the-rise-in-colombia.
9. http://www.diplomatmagazine.com/index.php?option=com_content&view
=article&id=538&Itemid=.
10. wcdirect1.ijet.com/direct/tir/DemoGenTIR.public?id=196&city=Brazil.
11. https://www.osac.gov/Pages/ContentReportDetails.aspx?cid=13966.
12. ezinearticles.com/?Executive-Protection---Hotspots&id=2631904.
13. Merco Press, Montevideo, January 10, 2014, 10:29 UTC.
14. http://travel.state.gov/content/passports/english/country.html.
15. http://www.worldtravelwatch.com/09/11/ecuador-kidnapping-threat-
blackouts-crime-in-quito.html.
16. http://ezinearticles.com/?Executive-Protection---Hotspots&id=2631904.
17. http://wn.com/kidnapping_en_haiti.
18. http://edition.cnn.com/2010/WORLD/asiapcf/12/09/taliban.refsdal.
qanda/index.html.
19. imgsecurity.net/kidnapping-part-ii-the-geography-of-the-crime.
20. http://www.smartraveller.gov.au/zw-cgi/view/advice/philippines.
21. http://news.bbc.co.uk/1/hi/world/asia-pacific/1354744.stm.
22. http://www.cidg.pnp.gov.ph/CrimeData.htm.
23. http://imgsecurity.net/kidnapping-part-ii-the-geography-of-the-crime/.
24. http://www.inkerman.com/assets/files/Kidnap%20%20Ransom%
20Monthly%20Review%20-%20July%202012.pdf.
25. https://www.osac.gov/pages/ContentReportDetails.aspx?cid=14130.
26. https://www.osac.gov/pages/ContentReportDetails.aspx?cid=13599.
27. https://www.osac.gov/Pages/ContentReportDetails.aspx?cid=12026.
28. http://www.inkerman.com/assets/files/Kidnap%20%20Ransom%
20Monthly%20Review%20-%20July%202012.pdf.

29. http://www.oceanprotectionservices.com/index.php/gulf-of-guinea.html.
30. http://www.inkerman.com/assets/files/Kidnap%20%20Ransom%20Monthly%20Review%20-%20July%202012.pdf.
31. http://erbil.usconsulate.gov/wm-041014.html.
32. https://www.gov.uk/foreign-travel-advice/nigeria.
33. http://www.upi.com/Top_News/Special/2013/05/10/Kidnapping-risk-high-in-Democratic-Republic-of-Congo/UPI-76881368195986/.
34. http://www.1cover.com.au/blog/travel-insurance/advice/guide-to-the-worlds-worst-travel-spots.html.
35. http://www.cfr.org/terrorist-organizations-and-networks/al-qaeda-islamic-maghreb-aqim/p12717.
36. https://www.osac.gov/pages/ContentReportDetails.aspx?cid=15067.
37. http://www.longwarjournal.org/threat-matrix/archives/2013/05/more_palestinian_kidnapping_pl.php#ixzz2r7yS7gRn.
38. http://www.bbc.co.uk/news/world-middle-east-11485774.
39. http://imgsecurity.net/kidnapping-part-ii-the-geography-of-the-crime/.
40. http://www.yementimes.com/en/1723/news/3038/Military-designs-new-uniform-to-thwart-terror.htm.
41. http://imgsecurity.net/kidnapping-part-ii-the-geography-of-the-crime/.
42. http://united-states.ezinemark.com/kidnapping-statistics-7d32e14fcdac.html.
43. http://www.justice.gov/oig/grants/2012/g6012006.pdf.
44. http://united-states.ezinemark.com/kidnapping-statistics-7d32e14fcdac.html.
45. http://www.amren.com/news/2005/06/a_kidnap_a_day/.
46. http://www.theguardian.com/uk/2005/jun/22/ukcrime.prisonsandprobation1.
47. http://www.theguardian.com/uk/2005/jun/22/ukcrime.prisonsandprobation1.
48. https://www.osac.gov/Pages/ContentReportDetails.aspx?cid=12108.
49. http://www.terrorism-info.org.il/data/pdf/PDF_06_234_2.pdf.

3

Attack Recognition and Personal Security Strategies

It is of great importance when traveling in high-risk kidnap countries that travelers, executives, and workers take primary responsibility for their own safety and security. Many of these high-risk countries have poor policing, and there is a limit to what local governments in these countries can do when a kidnap occurs.

Adapting behavior to make those at risk more of a problem for kidnappers can be easily achieved. For example:

- Keep a low profile.
- Alter personal routines.
- Avoid corporate tags on luggage, as these will advertise to a kidnapper that you are traveling on business.
- Dress sensibly. Avoid wearing expensive suits (see Figure 3.1) but also avoid looking like a tourist. No traveler's sandals, shorts, and baseball caps.
- Avoid areas where kidnappers are known to operate.
- Travel by air rather than road in kidnapping hotspots.
- Avoid "bush" or illegal taxis, and never flag down a cab yourself, especially when out on the street. Always ask your business manager or hotel to call an official taxi service. Women are much easier targets for kidnappers in these circumstances.
- Avoid street markets and nightclubs, as they are easy target areas for kidnappers to operate in.

Figure 3.1 Avoid wearing expensive suits or otherwise standing out. If they think you have money, kidnappers will look to profit from you.

- If going for a run, check with the hotel desk to ensure that your intended route is through a safe area (see Figure 3.2).
- Stay at a local hotel rather than an expensive American chain.
- Unless you are expecting a call, it is inadvisable to answer hotel internal speaker requests.
- Avoid wearing anything that identifies you as a business executive. For example, do not carry corporate bags or wear badges.
- Use your own credit card when making bookings, not a business one.
- When shopping, travel with an experienced local from the company or hotel who knows the areas to shop, especially when buying souvenirs. Your being lured into a shop is an open invitation to a kidnapper.
- Choose a standard car rather than a large upmarket one, and avoid "blacked out" windows. It is also preferable for the vehicle to be in a somewhat less than pristine condition.
- When traveling with the family, always hire a driver through the hotel or the office manager. The family will present an easy target for kidnappers.
- If on a long-term contract, try to integrate into local communities by learning the local language.

Figure 3.2 If sightseeing or going for a run, check with the hotel desk to ensure that your intended route is through a safe area.

Understanding one's potential as a kidnap victim and managing that risk through security strategies can significantly reduce the potential for being kidnapped. This is an area of policy that holds much potential for companies operating overseas offices, but it has, surprisingly, received relatively little attention.

It is possible to map the forces at work that drive economic kidnapping; for example,

- Where it occurs
- Who is involved
- Whom kidnappers target
- What motivates them

More important, it is possible to understand the interrelated influences that affect the economics of kidnapping and what drives them. Once this is understood, it is then possible to place the risks and rewards for kidnappers within a context covering the kidnapping organizations and the opportunities for the crime. Understanding these motivations can assist those at high risk to identify problem areas and categorize what changes need to be made to reduce the potential for being kidnapped.

Understanding the economic drivers of kidnap underlines the fact that while the crime and its causes have many interconnected foundations, it is possible to apply logic to the problem and effect a suitable strategy. Although an effective solution to the underlying causes of economic kidnapping may never be found, it is possible for potential victims to make themselves more difficult targets and thus lower the opportunities for the crime.

In 1999, the United States introduced the Combined Code on Internal Control (CCIC).[1] The CCIC and its subsequent recommendations on risk appraisal and management underlined the continued risk to the business community in respect to the crime of kidnapping.

Corporate organizations need to be acutely aware of their risk of kidnapping and act to reduce the risk and manage it accordingly. All companies listed on the London Stock Exchange are required to report their audited risk of kidnapping and whether they have taken the necessary steps to reduce their exposure to this type of crime.

Security is one element of an effective risk management strategy that can considerably reduce people's risk of being kidnapped. But attention generally tends to be focused on what measures and techniques can be employed on the ground. Companies must decide on and implement those risk management strategies that are likely to mitigate or prevent those incidents.

The relationship between companies working in kidnapping hotspots and their own governments needs to be clearly defined. Effective security systems and tactics to tackle kidnapping obviously require accurate and up-to-date intelligence regarding kidnapping trends, the groups concerned, and the groups' connections and political or religious beliefs. These systems should also be aware of the methodology utilized by various terrorist, political, and religious kidnapping groups, together with any political and economic developments in the country that might have a bearing on the incidence and type of kidnapping crime. Unfortunately, national governments are generally the keepers of such statistical data, and although it makes sense for them to coordinate a system for the dissemination of such data, this is not always the case.

At present, all companies can see information on the potential kidnap risk within the public domain via the web, but this is rarely up to date. Individuals, especially those with a background in the security business, may be able to obtain more detailed information through personal or professional contacts, but this is not always the case. Governments, because of their ponderous bureaucracy, can often act as a block to the dissemination of up-to-date information to those potentially at risk.

The governments of countries listed as being high-risk areas should examine initiatives such as the Overseas Security Advisory Council (OSAC),[2] which was established by the U.S. Department of State in 1984. The OSAC is dedicated to collaborating with U.S. companies on security issues, including abduction and kidnapping. The directive for the OSAC is from the business community itself.

The OSAC model may not be perfect for all governments, but it could offer useful ideas to be explored, especially in relation to kidnap and other crimes affecting large corporations in the gas and oil industry, as well as the general travel industry.

Companies and governments have distinct obligations for the management, safety, and security of their staff and citizens, but the risk of kidnapping is not restricted within the normal working hours of 9 to 5. Kidnappers in general strike when their victims are most exposed, such as when they are in the car between home and work and traveling at night.

When working in hotspot countries, individuals must, therefore, put the majority of the responsibility on themselves for their nonworking hours if they are to protect themselves and their families. This is not to remove the responsibility for the prime duty of care from their employers but rather to ensure that the right information is disseminated to their staff and guidance is given that they are able to look after themselves when they are not at work. In Brazil, for example, express kidnapping is the most common form of kidnapping. This is where victims are temporarily kidnapped and forced to make large withdrawals of money from cash points (ATMs). In such instances, regular briefings and sensible travel advice on the changing methodology of the various criminal groups and their areas of operation can assist employees in reducing the risk of kidnapping by changing their routine and/or behavior. A coherent system for disseminating information across a company and within travelers and travel companies will greatly assist in minimizing the risk of kidnapping.

There are many aspects that can influence the perception of personal risk, including family status, age, sex, and previous overseas living experiences. Companies with overseas staff must find appropriate ways of communicating these threats with different individuals and diverse groups.

Those who are overseas with their family either traveling or in business are more inclined to become security aware and are, therefore, more amenable to information and advice about risk management. The logic of this is "the more one has to lose, the more inclined one will be to embrace self-awareness and self-protection strategies."

Given that the traditional long-contract expatriate is now making way for new styles of business traveler, including international commuters, frequent flyers, and gap-year students and short-term travelers, this poses a significant challenge for companies in disseminating the risks to those concerned. Governmental foreign offices should be able to bridge this gap, but, as mentioned before, the bureaucracy of these large civil service departments renders the dissemination of up-to-date material and advice unlikely.

For companies, having a clear structure in place to deliver this information and associated warnings is important on two levels. First, it enables employees to take better control of the security for themselves and their families and dependents. Second, it allows companies to show that they have fulfilled their duty of care to their staff, both within and outside of office hours.

It must be remembered that the probability of being kidnapped is very small. If it does happen, the chances of survival are, unless it is a jihadist kidnapping, high. It should also be remembered that the victim is nothing more than of monetary value to the kidnapper. However, this is only so as long as the victim is alive, and the kidnapper will want to keep it that way.

If you are kidnapped, your best defense and chance of survival is passive cooperation. The greater the passage of time, the greater the chances are that you will be released alive. As for resisting being kidnapped, it should be remembered that the vast majority of people are very poorly prepared for such an incident. Most people have no idea how to defend themselves against even the most amateurish mugger, let alone a well-organized and determined kidnapper.

Unfortunately, people tend to think that what they see in films and TV programs can be achieved by the average man on the street. An organized kidnapper or armed attacker will have the element of surprise on his side, and the victim will be overpowered in a matter of seconds. Even a person experienced in martial arts will have little or no chance against a surprise attack, especially if the assailant is armed.

As Juan A. Garcia Jr. stated in his article "Attack Recognition" in *The Panama News*, "No matter how many personal security, or martial arts classes you take if you can not [*sic*] recognize pre-threat indicators prior to a kidnapping ... the chances of you avoiding, deterring, and surviving an attack are limited."

Preattack recognition is one of the most important tenets in any personal security stratagem. Being able to correctly identify whether a person's movements indicate that a dangerous situation is developing is vital if one is to avoid and escape from a hostile situation. Attack recognition is, in short, the mental preparedness necessary to reacting to an attack. When prethreat indicators are recognized, avoidance maneuvers that have been practiced in advance can be employed to counter the attack and escape.

Criminals will always have a number of advantages over their victims, as they will have preplanned the attack and be able to select the target, time, and location for the kidnap. Analyzing current kidnapping methodology, preplanning security responses, and being alert and aware of your surroundings at all times will significantly reduce any advantages a criminal will have. Included in these steps is positively reacting once it is felt an attack is imminent. Once the attack is in progress, this anticipatory phase is lost for good, and the end result is predictable.

Analyzing the trends in such kidnapping incidents is crucial. Important aspects in these analytical considerations include the following:

- Are more attacks occurring at night?
- Are the attacks random or targeted at a certain type of person?
- Is traveling roads at certain times becoming increasingly dangerous?
- Which roads are proving to be more dangerous?
- Are particular makes and models of cars being targeted?
- Are persons of a particular nationality being targeted more frequently than others?
- Are attacks being committed by multiple individuals or by single attackers?
- Are the attacks being carried out on a random basis, or is there some underlying approach to the selection of target, time of day, location, and so on?
- Are weapons being utilized, and if so what types of weapons are being used?

Only if you are able to identify an impending attack will the criminal be placed at a distinct disadvantage. Your recognition of prethreat indicators is something the kidnappers would not have anticipated or be prepared for.

A positive identification of the intended target must be made prior to an attack if the act is to be successful. This will normally involve the kidnappers giving away their intentions by focusing too much on the target or by signaling another attacker of the impending target. Such indicators are easy to spot once one is aware of their presence.

Asking for directions, a cigarette, or change are methods often utilized to disguise an impending attack. These subterfuges can easily be identified, as the attackers will usually be in an enhanced state of tension, scanning the area or nervously engaging in conservation while hiding their mouths from view. When more than one attacker is utilized, one will often make himself or herself obvious to the victim so that the victim's attention is solely focused on that individual while another kidnapper attacks from another direction.

You should become competent at recognizing movement patterns that might reveal a potential kidnap situation. Important factors that you should be able to recognize include the following:

- When you notice someone is looking at you but who then suddenly looks away when his or her interest is recognized
- When you are crossing a street, an individual moves directly toward you or at an angle
- While driving you observe a following car, generally one or two vehicles behind, taking the same route
- You observe someone lurking in the shadows outside your premises, work garage, or parking area
- You get unexpected "room service" in a hotel
- An unusual interest is being taken by office staff in your appointments diary

If you feel that something is not right, it usually means it is not, and in these situations you must trust your intuition and instincts. At this juncture, a move to a more advantageous position at the first possible instance is a priority, and implementation of one or more of the following is strongly advised:

- Placing some object, a car for instance, between you and the criminal is essential, and at this stage you should make every possible attempt to separate yourself from the attacker.

- It must not be forgotten that a kidnapper has to move toward the victim to execute an attack. Being alert and aware of any correlation of movement will place you in a position to recognize pre-threat indicators and respond positively.
- The ability to exploit the inflexibility of the kidnappers' modus operandi is paramount. If the attack is planned, for example, in a dark car park, but you recognize this, your crossing the street while moving in a different direction will exploit the attacker's probable lack of preparation and ability to execute a change in plan.
- If, while you are enjoying a relaxing day of shopping, you observe the same individual or individuals at various locations, street intersections, and so on, this is probably not a coincidence. A need to focus on a response to this situation is essential. If your pre-attack awareness intuition is in a heightened state and indicates that things are not right, trust your intuition, as things are probably not. Many victims of attacks later admitted that their instincts were warning them something was not right, but because they disregarded these warnings, the outcome was a successful kidnap.

Being able to trust your intuition, correlate the movements of suspicious-looking individuals, and react proactively are your keys to survival. Remember that if your instincts are indicating that you are in a potentially dangerous situation where you are likely to be kidnapped, then you must trust those instincts, react appropriately, and move toward safety. It is immaterial whether you're walking or driving; you must always trust your intuition.

GENERAL SECURITY TIPS

- Notify your family, friends, or company of your whereabouts while traveling.
- Leave information regarding your expected time and date of return.
- On arrival at your destination, register with your embassy.
- Inquire from your embassy about the latest security advice and information regarding high-threat areas. Embassy security officers are usually more than happy to inform travelers.

- You can deter a thief from targeting you simply by appearing to be alert and confident.
- Do not speak in a loud voice, especially in non-English-speaking areas.
- Avoid discussing your travel plans in bars, hotel lobbies, and other public areas where they may be overheard.
- If possible, use less than pristine luggage.
- Cover with a flap any luggage tags with your name, address, and destination.
- Don't mark your keys with your name and address.
- Do not take your hotel keys with you when you leave the premises, but deposit them with the reception desk.
- Do not carry a laptop in open view or in a bag recognizable as such. A backpack is always preferable.
- Vary your routines and daily routes.
- Do not wear logos that reveal your company or nationality.
- Always avoid out of the way areas and streets.
- Avoid civil disturbances and demonstrations.
- Do not discuss or become involved in local politics or any political activity.
- Avoid red-light districts and down-market clubs, especially at night.

In Restaurants, Bars, and Nightclubs

- Stay alert and avoid excess alcohol consumption.
- Ensure that you never leave your drink unattended, even when you visit the toilet.
- Avoid accepting food or drink from strangers. The drugging of food is an increasing concern in some countries.
- Without being rude, avoid overly friendly locals who may want to introduce you to a "special" restaurant or shop.

Personal Belongings

- Consider using a clip for your money rather than a wallet that will contain all your cards and other personal data. If you have your money in a clip and you are robbed, the only thing you will lose is the money in the clip. Your credit cards will remain secure in the hotel or company safe.

- If you must carry a wallet, place a thick rubber band around it. The additional friction between the rubber band and a trouser or coat pocket will make it much more difficult to remove without your knowledge.
- Always ensure that your wallet is carried in a pocket with a zip or button closure. If this is not possible, carry your wallet in a front pocket, as it is all but impossible to remove it from this location surreptitiously.
- Reduce your wallet or purse contents, particularly credit and debit cards, cards denoting affiliations, memberships, accounts, and so on.
- If you will not be using your checkbook, don't bring it, let alone carry it around with you.
- Wear well-fitting clothes that allow freedom of movement rather than clothes that are overly tight or excessively baggy.
- Wear well-fitting shoes rather than loose-fitting ones or flip-flops. Ill-fitting shoes or flip-flops will make it that much more difficult if you have to run to escape.
- Consider carrying a personal/rape alarm.
- Dress down when you are out of the office. An expensive suit will advertise your worth as a valuable kidnap target. On the other hand, do not look like a vagrant, as this could attract attention from the local authorities.
- Always, always trust your instincts. If you feel something is not right or that you are uncomfortable in any situation, leave immediately.
- Take extra care in protecting mobile phones and laptop computers. These not only contain all your valuable personal and business data but also are favorite items of thieves and burglars around the world.
- Laptops can be taken from hotel rooms, vehicles, the street, your office, and even official residences.
- Ensure that your laptop and office computer have strong password protection.
- Always back up everything on your phone and laptop to a memory stick.
- Make copies of all important documents and your passport, credit cards, driver's license, travel itinerary, and travel tickets and any other pertinent paperwork. Keep all the originals in the hotel or office safe.
- Likewise, keep the contact numbers for banks, airlines, and embassies in case of theft.

- Typical "tourist" wear can include belt packs, traveler's sandals, shorts and T-shirts, and small day sacks. These will all make you stand out as a kidnapping target.
- In certain parts of the world, iPods, mobile phones, and certain clothing styles are everyday items, but in others they can make you stand out more than anything else.
- Dress discreetly.
- Use a belt wallet to carry your money and valuables.
- Unless they are covered up, do not wear expensive jewelry or watches on the streets. These advertise your worth for ransom.
- If you are being met at the airport by a car and driver, make sure that you know your contact's name and company. It could be anyone holding up a piece of card with your name on it.

When Out Walking or Shopping

- Crowded streets, local markets, and tourist areas are always a high-kidnap-threat area, as are public transport vehicles and bus stations.
- Be cautious when getting off a bus or train.
- Be careful if someone approaches you and asks for help or directions.
- A disturbance that draws everyone's attention could be a ruse to draw attention away from you and place you in a vulnerable position.
- Take caution if surrounded by a crowd.
- Do not stand on the street corner with a map, trying to find out where you are. Try to memorize your route beforehand.
- Use the airport tourist information office rather than ask a taxi driver for assistance.
- Exploit the knowledge of local drivers employed by your company or hotel.
- Avoid unlit or isolated areas and streets.
- If there is a large gathering of people, civil disturbance, or demonstration, move out of the area as quickly as possible.
- Do not engage in discussions about local politics with strangers, taxi drivers, or people you have just met.
- Avoid walking alone. It is always advisable to travel in groups of two or more.
- Take notice of your surroundings and anyone who is close to you. You might then be aware if anyone is following and will have already determined an escape route.

- Walk confidently at a steady speed and on the side of the street facing traffic. In this way you will see approaching cars and who is inside the vehicle.
- Avoid doorways, bushes, and alleys.
- As you walk to your car, have the keys in your hand. Not only will this enable you to enter the car quickly, but the keys will provide you with a weapon should it be needed.
- As soon as you are in the car, lock all the doors and close the windows.
- Avoid wearing headphones turned up loud. This will enable you to hear what is happening around you.
- Avoid waiting for long periods at train stations and bus stops by checking timetables in advance. If there is no other option and you have to wait, try to stand near other people and in a well-lit area.
- When you are traveling in a bus, always try to sit or stand near others or near the driver. Never enter an empty bus or train carriage alone.
- Take notice of who gets off at your stop and attempt to determine whether he is following you.

In the Hotel

- Before arriving at your hotel, ensure that you have ascertained the emergency services' capabilities and fire escape routes.
- Always select a hotel room between the third floor and the fifth floor. Higher floors may be out of reach of fire equipment, but kidnappers can often gain access to the lower floors via fire escapes and external staircases from the outside.
- When checking in at your hotel, ensure that the hotel clerk does not say out loud your room number. Instead, request that the clerk write the room number down for you. If he or she does say the number out loud and you don't feel comfortable, request a change to a different room.
- Ensure that the hotel garage does not have elevators taking passengers to guest floors. It should go only to the lobby.
- When arriving in your room, turn on all lights and inspect the room and make sure all the locks on the windows and balcony doors are secure and in working order.

- Make sure that the lock on the room door functions properly and that there is an internal method of locking the door, such as a security door chain or sliding bolt, as well. If none is present, a rubber wedge placed under the door or even a chair placed underneath the handle is effective in securing the door from the inside.
- Make sure any doors to adjacent rooms are locked and secure.
- Ensure that the curtains close completely.
- If a "Do Not Disturb" sign is provided in the room, immediately place it on the outside of your door.
- When going to your room, have your key out when you leave the elevator.
- Use the door "spy hole" before opening the door to visitors.
- Always make sure that all doors, including balcony sliding glass doors, are locked at all times. If the curtains are drawn, it is easy to miss an unlocked window.
- Whenever you have arranged to meet someone in a hotel, always arrange to meet in the hotel lobby, not on the street outside.
- Don't leave your room key visible on a restaurant table or bar.

When Driving or Being Driven

- Avoid traveling in high-status cars. A Mercedes 600SL might be the ultimate businessman's transport, but it advertises your kidnap and ransom potential.
- At all costs avoid taxis on the street in kidnap hotspots.
- Do not use unmetered taxis.
- In higher risk areas, use only taxis booked through a restaurant or your hotel.
- Never share a taxi with anyone you do not know.
- In high-threat areas, prearrange transportation with a driver who is familiar with local driving conditions.
- In very high-risk areas, try to hire a driver trained in defensive tactics. In such extreme situations, it may be necessary to travel in a convoy, keeping in touch via mobile or satellite phone.
- Even if there isn't an air conditioner in the vehicle, keep your vehicle doors locked and windows up.
- When stationary, do not roll down your window. If someone approaches, drive away quickly even if it means running a red light.

- When stopped at traffic lights, be especially aware of street sellers or windshield cleaners.
- When stopped at traffic lights, leave ample maneuvering space between your vehicle and the one in front. Two meters is the absolute minimum to allow you to drive around the vehicle in front without reversing.
- Be especially alert when leaving from or arriving at your destination, as these are very high-risk locations for kidnap.
- When arriving at your destination, if it has a security gate, do not pull right up to the gate, waiting for the guard to open it. Kidnappers can either drive up and block the car from behind or simply surround the car, dragging you out of the car or driving off with you inside. In such a serious situation, shots are likely to be fired to scare away would-be rescuers. This can be a very serious and frightening experience.
- While you are driving, would-be kidnappers may point at your tires, shouting for you to stop because the tire is flat. Once the car has stopped, you will be at the mercy of the kidnappers.
- If you think you are being followed or watched, drive around a block a couple of times. This will identify anyone who is following.
- If another driver attempts to drive you off the road, do not stop. Do everything you can to escape, even if it means ramming the other car. Drive straight to a police station or some other area with an armed security presence.
- If you are being followed, try to make a note of the license plate and the make and color of the car. This may be difficult if you are trying to get away at a high speed.
- If you have a mobile phone and can use it, do so. If you don't, pretend to use a mobile phone with something of similar shape and size.
- As soon as you have reached a safe place, get inside as fast as possible, and do not worry about parking illegally.
- If you are being followed and are involved in an accident, do not stop to exchange insurance and other information, as it could be a trap. Drive straight to a police station, and if that is not possible, drive to a public place with a telephone and call the police from there. It is preferable that you check with your embassy beforehand to ascertain whether this advice is appropriate for the country you are visiting. Not all police forces have the same degree of credibility.

- When parking, look for somewhere that is well lit and close to somewhere that is busy. Consider whether it will be safe and still well lit when you are scheduled to return to the car.
- Always try to reverse into a parking place, as this will allow for a speedy exit when you return.
- If you have a flat tire or the car breaks down, tie a handkerchief or some other flag-like object to the radio aerial or trap a newspaper in the driver's door window and lock all the doors. When someone stops to help, do not get out of the car unless it is the police. It may be considered impolite, but if it is someone other than a personal friend or the police, speak to him or her through the closed window.
- If you are in an open air car park or parked on the street and have trouble with the car, be wary of personal assistance from strangers. Use your mobile phone to call a repair service or friend for assistance.
- If you feel threatened by strangers standing close to your car, lock the doors and close the windows. Sounding the horn will attract attention and, it is hoped, scare away a would-be kidnapper.
- Roadblocks or checkpoints are common in some countries and are often illegal. Approach them slowly, as these could be potential kidnap locations. Switch off the headlights (leaving the side lights on) and turn on the inside light, so those manning the roadblock can clearly see you. Be very careful to avoid sudden movements, and keep your hands visible at all times. Do not reach down or to the glove box, as this could be misconstrued as your reaching for a weapon. Only move when you are told to retrieve ID, a driver's license, or some other document. Do not back the car up or try to avoid the roadblock, as officers will regard this as suspect and most probably open fire. Ensure you have your ID, driver's license, and insurance readily available. Be compliant and courteous no matter how you are treated.

At Home

- At your home address, ensure that all doors and gates have high-quality locks fitted. These should preferably be of the deadbolt type (key with a flag), as these are much more difficult to pick that the normal "Yale"-type cylinder locks. It is also impossible to use a credit card to push back the locking bolt with this type of lock.

- All doors to the outside should also be fitted with at least one slide bolt. Safety chains can be of use, but unless they are well fitted, they can be next to useless. If the chain has too much movement, an intruder can often put his hand around the door and disengage the chain. If the screws are of insufficient length or made of insubstantial material, a shoulder to the door will often be more than sufficient to pull out the fixings.
- All inside doors should have substantial slide bolts fitted so that if an intruder breaks in, you can retreat into a panic area.
- Keep doors locked and ensure bolts are slid across when you are at home.
- Install window locks on all windows and ensure that the glass is of the toughened type. Toughened glass, especially if installed as double glazing, is much more difficult to break than standard glass.
- To prevent the power being turned off, have locks fitted to all fuse boxes. Being plunged into darkness can be extremely dangerous.
- Don't leave keys hidden outside the home under flower pots or such like. Any competent criminal will be able to locate them in seconds. Leave a spare key with a trusted neighbor or colleague or in your work safe.
- Know your neighbors and develop a neighborhood watch system. Develop a relationship with them and offer to keep an eye on each other's homes.
- Do not put your name on your mailbox and if possible ensure that you are not listed in the telephone book.
- If a stranger phones asking for you by surname, ask for a first name. If the caller cannot provide it, hang up and call the authorities.
- Locks must be changed even if just a single key is lost.
- If there is a change in domestic staff, a change of locks will be essential, especially if you parted under less than ideal circumstances.
- Windows and balconies should be fitted with steel bars, and special attention should be paid to any balcony or window near an adjoining roof.
- Properties close to the center of town will be safer than those in the suburbs. Those close to a police or military base will be safer still.
- If you are living in a house, it should be protected with ten-foot-high (3.05 meters) wire fencing preferably topped with razor wire. If the house is surrounded by fencing, paint antivandal paint along the top edge and down the outside.
- Pedestrian and garage doors should be of metal construction.

- The car-entry point should have an automatic garage door opener, with controls both in the car and inside the house.
- Automatic garage doors must have a manual opening facility in case of power cuts.
- All gates should have spy holes or preferably closed-circuit television (CCTV) coverage. CCTV should be on a recording loop so that if an incident occurs, the recording can be viewed at a later date.
- When setting up a safe room in your home, ensure that it is an internal room. Install a two-way communications system, telephone, or mobile phone and furnish the safe haven with a first aid kit, some essential supplies such as water and tinned food, and, if appropriate, a weapon.
- When planning to travel, notify your embassy's security office of your travel plans and the departure and return dates.
- When traveling, leave contact numbers with trusted people in your office.
- Before departing, check outside lighting and replace older light bulbs that might burn out while you are away.
- Household staff and family members should be reminded to keep a lookout for anyone suspected of keeping the property under surveillance, attempts to gain access to your residence by dishonest means, and telephone calls requesting personal information.
- Instruct family members and household staff to note descriptions and license numbers of any suspicious vehicles.

Detecting Surveillance

- Surveillance is used to identify a potential kidnap target based on the security precautions that have been taken and the most suitable time, location, and method to accomplish the abduction.
- Surveillance may last for just a couple of days or several weeks.
- Detecting surveillance and recognizing those concerned requires a constant state of alertness and awareness of your surroundings and will eventually become second nature for travelers in hotspot areas.
- A sense of what is considered to be normal in the country you are operating in and what is unusual in your surroundings may be far more important than any other type of security precaution you may take. As stated previously, if you are unsure, do not hesitate to report any unusual event.

- If your routine means that you leave your home and office at the same time each day and take the same or most direct route, that will make it much easier for anyone to keep you under surveillance.
- You must frequently vary the route you take, times of travel, and even mode of travel taken.
- Be familiar with your route and ensure that you not only have alternate routes to take but also have escape routes that you have preplanned.
- Most attacks will take place near your residence, as that part of the route is least easily varied.
- You are more vulnerable in the morning when departing for work than in the evening when returning from work. Evening return times vary because of unavoidable late working or meetings and so on and are less predictable than the morning departure time.
- Many surveillance teams use vans with one-way windows that permit observation from the interior of the van but make it all but impossible to see in from the outside. Magnetic false business labels can be easily obtained and will provide some pretext for the vehicle being in the area.
- Be aware of anyone dressed in a public utility uniform, telephone repair people, or road workers who might be working near your home or office. These could well be kidnappers in disguise.
- A common ploy used to keep someone under surveillance is to use women and children to give an appearance of innocence.
- If you have even the slightest suspicion that you are being followed, drive to the nearest police station or your consulate.
- Don't wait to verify that you are under surveillance before reporting your suspicions to the authorities. If you wait to make sure, then it could well be too late.
- Always check your vehicle inside, outside, and underneath before entering it. An inspection mirror on a telescopic rod is useful for checking underneath a vehicle. If there is anything suspicious, such as a packet fixed underneath, do not get in the car under any circumstances.

To Sum Up

Be alert, watch for unusual patterns of movement of those around you, and use your built-in sense of danger and act on it if something feels wrong.

53

ENDNOTES

1. *Internal Control: Guidance for Directors on the Combined Code*, www.ecgi.org/codes/documents/turnbul.pdf.
2. Overseas Security Advisory Council (OSAC), http://www.state.gov/m/ds/terrorism/c8650.htm.

FURTHER READING

http://www.thepanamanews.com/pn/v_12/issue_21/business_02.html.
"Kidnapping Part IV: Avoidance—10 Tips," http://imgsecurity.net/kidnapping-part-iv-avoidance-10-tips/.
"Kidnap Avoidance for Executives," http://www.imac-training.com/catalog.php?item=20.
"Kidnap Prevention," http://aftershockcem.wordpress.com/tag/kidnap-prevention/.
"Kidnap Avoidance and Survival," www.closeprotectionworld.com.
"Surviving Kidnapping," http://danger.mongabay.com/kidnapping.htm.
"Executive Protection: Basic Kidnap Avoidance," goarticles.com/article/Executive...Basic-Kidnap-Avoidance/1857549.
Richard P. Wright, *Kidnap for Ransom: Resolving the Unthinkable* (Auerbach, 2009).
Diana M. Concannon, *Kidnapping: An Investigator's Guide*, 2nd ed. (Elsevier Insights, 2013).
Aaron Doyle, Randy Lippert, and David Lyon, *Eyes Everywhere: The Global Growth of Camera Surveillance* (Routledge, 2012).

4

Vehicle Selection

The vast majority of kidnappings occur from a vehicle. After mounting a lengthy surveillance, the kidnapper will either engineer an opportunity or just wait for one to happen naturally. This could be a traffic accident or while the victim is waiting at a traffic light or simply attempting to turn at a junction. The possibilities open to a determined kidnapper are endless, and it is of overriding importance that the balance is tipped away from the kidnapper and into the ambit of the victim.

Vehicle selection is crucial, as no single type of vehicle is going to address all of the requirements for anyone under threat of kidnapping. For example, a large SUV is a solid, powerful vehicle and able to drive its way through roadblocks. However, such vehicles are not suited for low-key avoidance movements or high-speed swerving because of the high ride height and bulk of this type of vehicle. In addition, being large and more identifiable, it is easier to detect and conduct surveillance on.

A basic nondescript largish sedan is a good choice as a low-key mode of transport for those worried about being under surveillance and threat of kidnap. There are, however, other options depending on the circumstances, level of threat, and determination of the kidnapper.

TIPPER TRUCK

In many very high-threat areas, the vehicle of choice utilized by private security contractors and military Special Forces for those under particular threat is a six-wheeled, fourteen- or eighteen-ton tipper truck. These vehicles, while not possessing the same top speed or acceleration as a 4 × 4 or large sedan, are quite rapid enough for most purposes. In addition, they are very robustly built, with much thicker steel being used in the cab panels and a very solid bumper for smashing its way through barricades.

Having a number of wheels fitted with very robust tires, they are far less likely to be deflated due to weapons fire or stinger-type deflators. If one of the tires is shot out, there are others on which the truck can continue to drive.

If armed aggressors are pursuing the truck, the tip-up back can be raised for added protection against small arms fire. The tip-up back can also be filled with several tons of 25 mm or 50 mm gravel that can be tipped onto the road or on top of a following vehicle should the occasion arise for such methods. Such a vehicle, especially if in a visually somewhat less than pristine condition, provides the perfect camouflage for a high-risk target.

4 × 4 SUV

Although a truck may be the ideal antikidnap vehicle, it is often not the most practical and only of real use for transporting anyone at threat from A to B through a very high-risk area. Having one parked outside of one's apartment or house is not going to be at all practical either. As a result, most of the time there is little left in the choice of a suitable vehicle other than a 4 × 4.

For an all-around ideal security vehicle, a large robust 4 × 4 SUV is probably the best choice overall. The larger, more off-road-oriented vehicles (preferably not the soft-roader class of SUV vehicle such as the RAV4, Fiat Panda 4 × 4, etc.) are very solidly built, generally have large powerful engines, can punch their way through barricades and vehicles blocking the road, have good off-road potential, and, generally, have a large luggage and personnel capacity.

The drawbacks of using such vehicles include their relatively low top speed, slow acceleration, and unsuitability for low-speed avoidance movements because of their bulk. There is also the potential for tipping over during high-speed swerving as a result of their high ground clearance. Another disadvantage of an SUV is the large target area it provides for small arms fire. This may not be of great importance in most kidnappings; however, a thwarted armed kidnapper may resort to such tactics in extreme circumstances.

PICKUP TRUCK

Nestling between a 4 × 4 and a sedan is the ubiquitous pickup truck. This would preferably be one with an extended cab enabling it to seat five people and have four-wheel drive.

As seen in use by all terrorists and insurgents (usually with a .50 Browning or 30 mm heavy machine gun mounted behind the cab), as well as used as bush taxis in third-world countries, pickup trucks are virtually indestructible. They have high ground clearance, powerful diesel engines, and a good turn of speed, and are constructed from very substantial steel. They are available in both two- and four-wheel drive, with four-wheel drive being preferable for adverse conditions. With an extended cab, they can accommodate five people together with a substantial amount of equipment or even armed guards in the open back.

SALOON

Large sedans definitely have their place, but high-end cars, such as the Mercedes SL600, Lexus LS600, and BMW 7 series, should be avoided. Such cars present an open invitation that someone inside is worth kidnapping for a large ransom. Having said that, using a small hatchback car of the Ford Fiesta or Honda Civic size is of little or no use. Such small cars are difficult to keep under surveillance in traffic and present a lower profile for small arms fire, but are not as robust, have smaller and less powerful engines, and are of little use in defeating roadblocks and barriers. In addition, if it is necessary to go off-road or mount curbs, they have little ground clearance and are likely to lose the engine sump and exhaust system on the curb. If a Mercedes or BMW is considered as the preferable mode of transport, then a C or E class Mercedes or a Series 3 or 5 BMW would be ideal. Whichever saloon is chosen, it should not be in pristine condition, as a dirty vehicle with the odd dent or scratch will be far less visible and easily blend in with local traffic. The selected vehicle should not have security (heavily tinted) glass, as, once again, this is an indicator that someone inside is worth kidnapping.

Whatever type of vehicle is chosen, consideration should be given to the fitting of puncture-proof tires. These will resist small arms fire and stinger-type tire deflators and enable the vehicle to be driven for thirty or forty miles at considerable speed even with several punctured tires.

ARMORING A VEHICLE AGAINST SMALL ARMS FIRE

As mentioned earlier, in most situations kidnappers do not resort to firing weapons at their intended target. They may have pistols, submachine guns, or assault rifles to intimidate or warn off potential rescuers, but shooting the target is definitely not the normal consideration for the kidnapper. Having said that, kidnappers thwarted by aggressive or defensive driving or having a gun pointed at them by the intended victim could result in the would-be kidnappers opening fire in an attempt to stop the vehicle. Unless a fully armored vehicle is available (see Figure 4.1), due consideration should be given to up-armoring the chosen vehicle.[1]

Armoring a vehicle is, however, a difficult area, as it is all but impossible to completely bulletproof a standard car and still have it capable of movement. If the doors are armored with, for example, Kevlar, then the window glass will be vulnerable. Making the window glass bullet

Figure 4.1   A close-up of a light armored vehicle.

resistant is extremely difficult and adds considerably to the weight of the vehicle.[2,3] With most terrorists using AK47s or some variant of this weapon, glass several inches thick is required to stop the 7.62 × 39 mm steel-cored bullet that this type of weapon normally fires. Not only is this glass going to be extremely heavy, but also unless it is specifically made for a make and model of vehicle, it can generally only be made in flat sheets. As would be expected, this is going to be extremely expensive.

In general terms, the likelihood of a handgun bullet, even from one of the more powerful pistols, getting through the door of a car is fairly slim. Side impact strengthening, window winder motors, locks, hinges, and so on all leave little room for a normal handgun bullet to completely penetrate the door. Bullets fired toward the rear of a vehicle will, however, have a much easier time in penetrating all the way through to the driver or front passenger, as the rear panel of the trunk and rear bulkhead are made of only relatively thin steel.

Up-armoring a vehicle is, as can be expected, a specialized and very expensive undertaking, with such modifications costing in the US$50,000 to US$100,000 range.[4] And this will probably provide bullet resistance only up to 7.62 × 39 mm AK47 (Kalashnikov) steel-cored ammunition. Anything more, such as armoring against an armor-piercing round from a military rifle or even a .50" Browning, will be inordinately expensive.

The range of materials available for such armoring is quite extensive, with new materials being developed all the time. At this juncture, it is worth delving into the history of bullet-resistant materials and how they have developed over the years.

HISTORY

During World War II, ballistic nylon (a copolymer of the basic polyamide) was used against shrapnel from grenades.[5] The specification used was an 18-ounce fabric manufactured from 1,050-denier high-tenacity nylon thread. Although it was effective against shrapnel, it was, however, of little use against bullets other than very low-velocity soft lead projectiles.

The major advance in soft body armor came with a generation of what are loosely referred to as *super fibers*. These were first introduced by DuPont in the 1970s. The best known of these was a para-aramid fiber

59

called Kevlar,[6] which was originally used in fabric-braced radial tires. It did not take long for it to be realized that these fibers could be woven into a fabric that was so strong that it could be used in bullet-resistant (never to be referred to as "bulletproof") soft body armor and for the armoring of vehicles, helicopters, and so on.

The Kevlar fibers were simply woven into sheets, with varying thicknesses of yarn and density of weave (called *denier*), to provide the particular properties required. The sheets were then assembled into ballistic panels by stitching them together. These panels were then permanently sewn into a carrier for the intended purpose. These panels could also be made rigid by soaking the pack of Kevlar sheets in an appropriate resin and allowing it to cure. By allowing the resin-soaked pack to set while it is draped over a former, intricate shapes such as the underside of a helicopter, seat shells, fuel tanks, or car seats can be produced.

It is undeniable that Kevlar does produce a very effective, lightweight, and flexible bullet-resistant material that can be tailored to stop virtually any handgun missile. It does, however, suffer from a number of problems. First, it is not stable to UV light and has to be kept inside a lightproof pouch. Second, it is very susceptible to attack by many household chemicals, and third, if wet (unless formed into a resin-based sheet) the normal flexible Kevlar sheets lose most of their ability to stop bullets.

A recent development in the field of bullet-resistant materials involves the use of an ultra-high molecular weight polyethylene fiber called Spectra produced by Allied Signal Inc.[7] or Dyneema produced by DSM.[8] Both products consist of exceedingly finespun fibers of polyethylene. These fibers are laid, in dense mats, at 90° to each other, then covered top and bottom with a thin sheet of polyethylene. This whole bundle is then heat-treated to semimelt the fibers together, or alternately they can be bonded with a plastic resin to form a sheet. With the thousands of bonded fibers that must be pulled apart to allow the bullet to penetrate, the sheets are far more efficient than Kevlar.

Spectra material is not affected by water (in fact it floats), it is not affected by UV light or any chemical, and it is considerably lighter than Kevlar. If it has a disadvantage, it is that its melting point is much lower than that of Kevlar, although this is not generally an issue.

One of the most recent innovations in bullet-resistant materials concerns the use of materials that exist as a semisolid under normal circumstances, but when they are subjected to a shock, such as a bullet strike, they solidify. These are called *shear thickening materials* (or dilat-ant materials) and are composed of hard particles suspended in a liquid.[9] The liquid is generally polyethylene glycol, and the particles are nano-sized pieces of silica. This shear thickening liquid is soaked into the layers of a normal pack of Kevlar. The pack so formed will have the same bullet resistance as a pack of standard Kevlar weighing at least a third more.

According to BAE Systems in Bristol, United Kingdom,[10] recent tests in which projectiles were fired at 300 m/sec into a pack of thirty-one lay-ers of untreated Kevlar and another pack of ten layers of Kevlar combined with the shear thickening liquid showed that the liquid-treated armor was as effective as the much thicker untreated one.

MECHANISM OF BULLET-RESISTANT MATERIALS

To effectively stop a bullet, the material must first deform the missile. If the surface area of the bullet is large enough and the material has suf-ficient resistance to the passage of the bullet, then the energy transfer to surrounding fibers can occur. A nondeformed bullet will merely push apart the weave and penetrate.

If the bullet is sufficiently soft, that is, plain lead, semijacketed, or thinly jacketed, then the material alone will often be sufficient to cause the deformation.[11] If, however, the bullet is heavily jacketed or of the metal-penetrating type, then some intermediate, much more rigid mate-rial will be required to first deform the bullet. This generally takes the form of a hard plate that fits in front of the soft body armor. This can be made from steel, tungsten alloy, heat-treated aluminum, or fused ceramic.

With a vehicle, the need for this intermediate hard plate is much reduced, as the bullet must first penetrate the steel body of the vehicle. Depending on the degree of up-armoring required, it may, however, in the case of highly penetrating rifle bullets, still require some form of thick intermediate plate.

The threat level posed by a particular type of missile and the type of armor required to defeat this is illustrated in Table 4.1, which provides the National Institute of Justice armor levels and the missiles that this level of armor will defeat.

Table 4.1 National Institute of Justice Armor Levels and the Missiles That the Level Will Defeat

Armor Level	Protection
Type I (.22LR; .380ACP)	.22 long rifle lead round nose (LRN) bullets at a velocity of 329 m/s (1,080 ft/s ± 30 ft/s) and 6.2 g (95 gr) .380 ACP full metal jacketed round nose (FMJ RN) bullets at a velocity of 322 m/s (1,055 ft/s ± 30 ft/s) (It is no longer part of the standard.)
Type IIA (9 mm; .40S&W; .45ACP)	9 × 19 mm parabellum FMJ RN bullets at a velocity of 373 m/s (1,225 ft/s) 11.7 g (180 gr) .40 S&W full metal jacketed (FMJ) bullets at a velocity of 352 m/s (1,155 ft/s) .45ACP FMJ bullets at a velocity of 275 m/s (900 ft/s)
Type II (9 mm; .357 Magnum)	9 mm FMJ RN bullets at a velocity of 398 m/s (1305 ft/s) .357 Magnum, jacketed soft point bullets at a velocity of 436 m/s (1,430 ft/s)
Type IIIA (.357SIG; .44 Magnum)	.357 SIG, FMJ flat nose (FN) bullets at a velocity of 448 m/s (1,470 ft/s) .44 Magnum, semijacketed hollow point bullets at a velocity of 436 m/s (1,430 ft/s)
Type III (rifles)	7.62 × 51 mm NATO, M80 ball bullets at a velocity of 847 m/s (2,780 ft/s) (It also provides protection against the threats mentioned in Types I, IIA, II, and IIIA.)
Type IV (armor-piercing rifle)	.30-06 Springfield M2 armor-piercing bullets at a velocity of 878 m/s (2,880 ft/s) (It also provides at least single hit protection against the threats mentioned in Types I, IIA, II, IIIA, and III.)

Note: See Appendix 6 for a list of bullet abbreviations.

UP-ARMORING THE BODYWORK OF A VEHICLE

This is a difficult area because of the complexities of installing the bullet-resistant materials, not to mention deciding on the level of protection required.

Installing ten or fifteen layers of Kevlar or Spectra sheets inside the doors would be a good start. This would, together with the window winders and side impact reinforcing girders, give more than adequate protection against most assault-rifle-type weaponry, including the AK47.

The rear bulkhead would need double the thickness of that installed in the doors, as this bulkhead is a fairly thin sheet of steel with none of the strengthening ribs or window winding mechanisms found in the doors. The front bulkhead would also need some additional protection despite having the engine in front of it.

As for the glassed areas, the following section is relevant.

BULLET-RESISTANT TRANSPARENT MATERIALS

Bullet-resistant glass (BRG) (see Figure 4.2) is designed to withstand one or more bullets depending on the construction of the glass composite and the caliber, velocity, and design of the bullet being fired at it. BRG comes in many forms depending on the manufacturer, but it is basically made by layering, with some type of adhesive, a polycarbonate material between

Figure 4.2 In the bullet-resistant glass shown, note the unique cracking that is different from that of traditional glass.

sheets of ordinary glass in a process called *lamination*. This laminated material has the same optical properties as glass but will defeat certain types of bullet depending on its thickness and the number of layers used. The interlaminate polycarbonate is a tough transparent plastic, known by various brand names including Lexan, Tuffak, Cyrolon, Makralon, and others.[12]

A bullet fired at a sheet of BRG will initially pierce the outside layer of the glass, deforming the bullet in the process. The layered polycarbonate glass material will keep the sheet intact and soak up the bullet's energy, stopping it before it exits the final layer. One of the problems with a glass/polycarbonate/glass-type structure is that the inside, i.e., nonstrike face, is plain glass that will "spall" when the strike face is struck by a bullet. Spalling is caused by the glass bulging away from the strike face and throwing shards of glass off the opposite nonstrike face. These shards of glass are traveling at a very high velocity and can cause serious injury or the death to anyone on that side of the glass. Spalling can be eliminated by bonding a thin sheet of polycarbonate to the nonstrike face, that is, the last layer of glass. The polycarbonate will effectively capture the shards of glass, preventing them from being spalled off. A problem with this type of glass/polycarbonate/glass/polycarbonate structure is that the nonstrike face of polycarbonate is very prone to scratching. Having said that, many of the more modern polycarbonates are quite scratch resistant.

Illustrative Case

A case that perfectly illustrates this problem occurred during a bank robbery where the bank tellers were protected by glass without this antispalling layer of polycarbonate. The robber, who was armed with a sawed-off 12 bore shotgun, shot the teller through the BRG. Although the shotgun pellets did not penetrate the glass, the spalling from the rear face was so severe that some of the shards completely penetrated the teller's body, killing her almost instantly. The photograph in Figure 4.3 shows the quantity of glass thrown off the rear face through spalling. This test firing was with the same gun used in the robbery and a sheet of identical glass as that used in the bank.

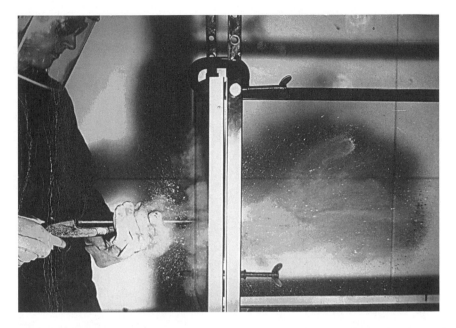

Figure 4.3 Glass fragments are thrown off the rear face (spalled) of a sheet of laminated glass that does not have an antispalling face.

Illustrative Case

Another case involved a more modern type of glass with a clear sheet of acrylic bonded to the nonstrike face. In this case, the bank teller had, completely illegally, taken his own .22″ caliber target pistol to work with him, "just in case his bank was robbed." The would-be robber was armed with a .38″ Special caliber revolver, which he waved in a threating manner at the teller. When the teller pulled out his own gun, the robber opened fire, as did the teller. When the smoke cleared, there were eight .22″ bullets from the teller's pistol embedded in the antispalling sheet and six completely smashed .38″ Special bullets lying on the floor by the robber's feet. The robber's hands and face had been cut to shreds by the shards of glass thrown back from the plain glass strike face of the glass, and he had to be taken to a hospital, with one eye missing and numerous severe lacerations to his face and hands.

Other problems with laminated BRG is that the thicker the laminate becomes, the greener and more opaque the glass becomes and the more difficult it is to produce curved sheets. A heavily up-armored vehicle is immediately recognizable by the dark green coloration of the glass and the flat or nearly flat contours of the windscreen glass. It is also inordinately heavy, and most vehicles will need uprated springs and nonopening windows.

MODERN DEVELOPMENTS IN TRANSPARENT BULLET-RESISTANT MATERIALS

Modern developments include a new type of BRG containing aluminumoxynitride (trade name ALON) as the strike face.[13] This type of glass composite has a much higher performance than traditional glass/polymer laminates. Because of the thinner layers that can be used in the laminate, it is also much lighter than conventional BRG. Depending on the construction, ALON BRG can defeat extremely penetrating rounds such as .50 caliber armor-piercing rounds, which would be almost impossible using traditional BRG.

Ceramic spinel is a class of mineral for transparent glass-type sheets and has increased density and hardness when compared to traditional glass.[14] These new types of synthetic ceramic transparent armors allow for thinner armor with an equivalent stopping power to that of traditional laminated glass.

Another recent development is one-way BRG.[15] One side of the sheet has the ability to stop bullets, and the other side allows bullets to pass through unaffected. This gives a person who is being shot at, for example, from inside a security van, an army checkpoint, police vehicle, or private car, the ability to shoot back.

One-way BRG is constructed with a brittle layer of glass on the outside bonded to a flexible polycarbonate-type material one on the inside. The brittle layer shatters and in doing so substantially damages the bullet's ballistics integrity and absorbs some of its kinetic energy (the energy the bullet possesses) while spreading it over a larger area. This process also reduces the velocity of the bullet. The bullet, now damaged and of considerably lower velocity and kinetic energy, is finally stopped by the flexible layer. However, a bullet fired at the inside, flexible layer easily penetrates this layer, then shatters the brittle layer outward because of the flexing of the inner layer, thus allowing the bullet to pass through relatively undamaged.

Rhino Glass by Armour Group Products Inc.[16] is one manufacturer of this type of glass, as is Total Security Solutions Inc.[17]

UP-ARMORING THE GLASS IN A VEHICLE

Up-armoring the glass of a vehicle is very difficult for a number of inter-related reasons.

Replacing the wind-down side window glass with a multilayer laminated glass is difficult for two reasons. First, the winding mechanism will almost certainly be unable to cope with the additional weight, and second, the gap through which the window slides up and down will be too narrow to take an uprated glass. These problems can be overcome but at great expense.

Replacing the glass with Makralon or some other bullet-resistant polycarbonate-type material is an alternative, but not if the window is to be opened. After just a few such openings, the polycarbonate will become scratched to the point where it becomes opaque. Windshield glass can be replaced with Makralon, as it is easily heat formed into curved profiles. It does, however, suffer from serious scratching by the windshield wipers.

Illustrative Case

In the 1970s, the undercover security forces in Northern Ireland were issued with a fleet or cars in which all the glass had been replaced with Makralon. After just a couple of weeks of use, the Makralon windows became so scratched that they were milky white and almost impossible to see out of.

Secondary glazing with the Makralon sheeting on the inside of the glass is a cheap alternative, but this has numerous problems, including the windows being unable to be opened, the inside surfaces becoming dirty, and, once again, the potential for scratching.

An alternative to fully BRG is a bullet-resistant film. In 2004, a company called Window Armour began selling a security film called Window Armour.[18] This laminate is usually made from a chemical called polyethylene terephthalate.

There are now many companies offering such a material, which is installed, by gluing, onto the inside of the vehicle's window and can protect against handheld weapons such as clubs and hammers, as well as more extreme weapons such as improvised explosive devices and hand grenades. With thicker layers of the film, low-powered handgun bullets can also be defeated.

It is generally available in various thicknesses from eight to twenty-two thousandths of an inch, depending on the type of protection required. It is also possible to apply the film to the outside surface of the window glass, which significantly increases its effectiveness.

For most purposes, a simple thin sheet of this security film is all that is required for antikidnap situations. As stated earlier, the kidnapper is not likely to want to kill the intended victim, as this action has, for the kidnapper, no monetary outcome. The kidnapper is more likely to try to force the victim out of the vehicle by smashing the glass with a baseball bat or hammer. In this type of situation, a single layer of security film is more than adequate. In more dangerous areas, however, more substantial up-armoring should be considered.

FULLY ARMORED VEHICLES

The commercial armoring of a vehicle is a complicated and expensive undertaking and will include the following:

- *Bodywork:* All areas of the bodywork will require up-armoring with additional sheet steel, tungsten alloy sheet, ceramic plates, or Kevlar or Spectra blankets. The Kevlar and Spectra could also be in the form of epoxy-bonded plates.
- *Floor protection:* Floors are protected with steel sheeting or rigid Kevlar panels concealed under the carpet to protect against explosions.
- *Roof protection:* Armor will be installed in the roof lining. This can be rigid or soft armor. If a sunroof is fitted, it will be replaced with Makralon or some such transparent armor. The opening mechanism is usually rendered inoperative in such a modification.
- *Fuel tank protection:* Most armored car companies protect the fuel tank by wrapping it with a Kevlar or preferably Spectra blanket.
- *Locking gas tank caps:* Fitting locking caps on the gas tank cap will prevent tampering with the fuel supply.
- *Battery protection:* Most armored car companies will replace acid, wet cell batteries with a lithium/ion type. Such batteries are

not at risk of exploding and causing damage to the engine and electonics via the leakage of battery acid.

- *Suspension upgrade:* As a result of the increased weight of the armor in the armored car, the suspension, shock absorbers, and brakes will often have to be replaced with uprated units.
- *Engine modifications:* As a result of the increase in the vehicle's weight, the power output of the engine will have to be substantially uprated. In some cases, it might even be necessary to replace the engine with one of much larger capacity and power.
- *Tire protection:* Tires can be protected against attack from small arms fire or stinger-type deflators in several different ways. One option is to have thick rubberized plastic rings placed inside each tire called a "run flat tire."[19] If the tire becomes deflated, the ring of hard rubber will allow the car to be driven for thirty or forty miles at quite high speeds.

Auto-inflated tires are another method of tire protection. Auto-inflated tires have an integrated air pump that keeps the tires inflated if they become deflated. This type of tire protection is, however, only for small punctures and would not cope with the tire being punctured by a stinger or shotgun fire. The tires in such systems can also be filled with a liquid sealant that immediately blocks any small punctures.

- *Bumper reinforcement:* This puts additional strength into the bumper and allows the armored car to drive its way through roadblocks and other dangerous situations. If the bumper is sufficiently reinforced, it will also prevent the corner of the bumper from being crushed into the tires when being used to ram its way out of trouble.
- *Door supports:* The transparent glass in the doors will weigh considerably more, requiring replacement and strengthening of the hinges, door risers, over extension straps, and so on.
- *Exhaust protection:* Wire mesh is required over the exhaust tail pipe to protect it from being blocked and stopping the engine.
- *Audible devices:* Some armored car companies also offer sirens, PA systems, and intercoms in their list of optional extras.
- *Gas protection:* Also offered is the option of an oxygen supply along with an airtight interior. This is to protect the occupants against gas or chemical threats.
- *Radiator protection:* Armoring around the radiator will be required to protect this vital engine component.

- *Transparent armor:* A glass/polycarbonate laminate can replace all the glass in the vehicle, including the windshield and all side and rear windows. With opening windows, the weight of the replacement armor generally means that they will no longer open. Some companies will, however, modify the doors and window opening motors so that they can still be opened.
- *Electrification of the vehicle's body:* By providing a large potential difference (50,000 volts or more) between the car and the ground, anyone attempting to touch the car will be immediately disabled. This can be a very effective deterrent, but the system must be grounded before exiting the vehicle!
- *Tear gas dispersion system:* If the hot exhaust system is sprayed with a liquid tear gas, a cloud of gas will surround the car thus preventing anyone approaching the vehicle. The interior of the car will, however, have to be sealed and provided with its own bottled air system to protect the driver and passengers.
- *Smoke generator:* The inclusion of a smoke generator either into the tear gas system or as a stand-alone generator will provide a cloaking smoke and/or gas cloud, allowing the vehicle to escape. Once again the cabin will have to be sealed and provided with its own bottled air system.

Not unsurprisingly, there is a relationship between the level of ballistic up-armoring and the additional weight that is placed on the vehicle. Armoring a car can add 2,000 pounds (907 kg) or even more to the vehicle's overall weight. This large additional weight will result in the car behaving very differently from an unmodified vehicle and will seriously affect the vehicle's acceleration, top speed, and stability when driven at speed.

As an example, the U.S. president's armored vehicle, which is based on a Cadillac DTS and called "The Beast," cost over one million U.S. dollars. It is 18 feet in length, weighs 8 tons, and has 8"-thick (20 cm) armor plating on its doors. It will defeat armor-piercing .50 Browning ammunition, grenades, and anti-tank rocket propelled grenades.

SOURCES

"Bullet and Impact Resistant Film," http://www.cjbuffer.com/, http://usace.com/products/.
"One-Way Ballistic Glass," http://www.tssbulletproof.com/one-way-ballistic-glass. http://www.thearmourgroup.com/pages/glass.html.

Laura Lundin, "Air Force Testing New Transparent Armor" (Air Force Research Laboratory Public Affairs, October 17, 2005).

P. E. Cros, L. Rota, C. E. Cottenot, R. Schirrer, and C. Fond, "Experimental and Numerical Analysis of the Impact Behaviour of Polycarbonate and Polyurethane Liner," *Journal de Physique IV France* 10 (2000): Pr9-671–Pr9-676.

Brian J. Heard, *A Handbook of Firearms and Ballistics: Examining and Interpreting Forensic Evidence*, 2nd ed. (Wiley Blackwell, 2008).

Rhino ONEWAY Glass, *www.thearmourgroup.com/pages/ram.html*.

Total Solutions One-Way Glass, www.tssbulletproof.com/bullet-proof-glass-disaster-preparedness.

ENDNOTES

1. www.dupont.co.uk/products-and-services/.../vehicle-armour.html.
2. www.romag.co.uk/architectural-glass/bullet-proof-glass.
3. www.tynesidesafetyglass.com/products/bullet-resistant-glass.html.
4. www.cararmorkits.com/.
5. http://en.wikipedia.org/wiki/Ballistic_nylon.
6. www.dupont.co.uk/products-and-services/fabrics-fibers.../kevlar.html.
7. csrbraids.com/index.php/spectra-fiber.html.
8. http://www.dyneema.com/.
9. dujs.dartmouth.edu/fall-2013/liquid-body-armor.
10. Sheer Thickening Materials BAE Systems, www.baesystems.com › Home › What We Do.
11. Brian J. Heard, *A Handbook of Firearms and Ballistics: Examining and Interpreting Forensic Evidence*, 2nd ed. (Wiley Blackwell, 2008).
12. science.howstuffworks.com/question476.htm.
13. science.howstuffworks.com/transparent-aluminum-armor3.htm.
14. www.armorline.com/.../ArmorLine%20Corp-Transparent%20Spinel%20.
15. www.tssbulletproof.com/one-way-ballistic-glass.
16. thearmourgroup.com/pages/ram.htm.
17. www.tssbulletproof.com/one-way-ballistic-glass.
18. Window Armour Film, www.armor-glass.com.
19. www.blackcircles.com › Tyres.

5

Defensive Driving

We would all like to believe that we are above average drivers. The truth is somewhat different, as the majority of us never get past the basics. Therefore, an understanding and knowledge of the more advanced techniques is extremely important when driving in hotspot kidnap areas.

The techniques employed in defensive driving are, in general, little more than what can be referred to as sensible driving. Such techniques, at their lowest level, allow a motorist to anticipate oncoming hazards and take appropriate action. It matters little whether these hazards are an error on the part of another driver, bad road conditions, or, at their most extreme, an attempt being made to stop or ram your vehicle.

Once people learn how to drive defensively, they will be able to improve their general driving skills, hazard perception, and reaction times. Naturally, defensive driving in a kidnap hotspot or terrorist situation involves much more than just being aware of your immediate surroundings.

Some of the more important details you need to master to become a more proficient driver include the following:

- Having a more preemptive attitude behind the wheel
- Anticipating likely hazards instead of simply reacting to them and then panicking
- Being aware of oncoming vehicles and those in front, by the side, and behind
- Ensuring that your vehicle is in the best possible position to safely escape from a situation

- Understanding a vehicle's potential top speed, acceleration, and handling abilities
- Understanding the concepts of *understeer* and *oversteer* and knowing how to correct and regain control of your vehicle should this become an issue
- Knowing how to maintain control of a vehicle while safely steering the vehicle past a hazard
- Knowing how to avoid, control, and drive out of a skid
- Knowing how to avoid road debris when driving at speed without rolling over
- Learning techniques to quickly change the direction in which your car is traveling by 180° (J-turns, U-turns, and handbrake turns)
- Minimizing damage to your vehicle during a car crash
- Knowing the correct way to mount curbs without seriously damaging the vehicle or its tires

Most of these techniques can be learned at various advanced driving schools, but the level of expertise is variable, and the techniques taught are not always applicable to everyday situations.

BASICS

Ensure that when you enter a car park, home parking area, or office car park you always have your keys in your hand. Valuable time can be wasted placing you in a potentially dangerous situation if you are fumbling around looking for the keys in a handbag or briefcase or sifting through the numerous pockets in a suit.

Look around for anything or anyone acting or looking suspect. If in any doubt that a criminal incident is about to happen, trigger the car's alarm system from the car's key fob. Potential kidnappers will always be alert for anyone watching, and the car alarm will bring unwanted attention to them and to you and your car. Such unwanted attention will normally be enough to have the kidnappers melting into the shadows.

The first thing to do when you get in the car is lock all the doors and make sure all the windows are completely closed. Start the car as soon as practically possible, put it in gear, look around again, and move the car out at least two feet (0.61 m) from its parked position. This will give you a better view up and down the road or car parking area, enabling you to better spot anything suspicious.

When you are slowing down to stop or moving in slow traffic, a distance of four feet (1.2 m) must always be left between your car and the one in front. This will enable you to pull out and overtake the car in front if a situation occurs. If you are too close, it will involve reversing, which will be impossible if there is a second car close behind.

A useful guide to judge this distance of four feet (1.2 m) is that you should be able to see the tires or at least the bumper of the vehicle in front of you. This will give you the required gap between the rear of the car in front and the front bumper of your car. This distance should be sufficient to pull around the car in front without additional maneuvers. Nowadays, however, many cars are manufactured with a sloping hood to comply with pedestrian impact regulations. In these cases, the front of the hood and front bumper may not be visible, making it difficult to judge the four-foot (1.2 m) gap. In these cases, some other reference point will have to be established so that the correct distance can be maintained without lifting yourself out of the seat to correctly gauge the distance.

One should, occasionally, check to determine whether another car is following. The following car could be one or two cars behind. If you have a suspicion that you are being followed, make a series of right turns until you are back on your original route. Driving through a supermarket car park will likewise immediately confirm whether you are being followed.

If a car is following, make a mental note of the car's make, model, and color and a description of the occupants and, if possible, its registration number. Noting the number plate may be difficult in those countries using Arabic or Cyrillic number plates.

Allowing those keeping you under surveillance to know that you have seen them is perfectly acceptable, but, as the U.S. Department of Agriculture recommends, do not, under any circumstances, take any aggressive action that might lead to a confrontation. Once they know you are aware that they are following you, they will probably just melt away. If they continue following you, drive directly to the nearest safe refuge. Police stations, military bases, and embassies are safe havens, and you should note their positions for any route taken. If you are being followed, *do not, under any circumstances, drive to your home.*

When planning a route, look for areas where the kidnappers can easily block you in (see Figure 5.1). If you feel any threat, ensure that you utilize another route that you have planned in advance.

Google Maps will show any potential problem areas in a planned route and will often give you a number of alternative routes. Driving

Figure 5.1 Look for, and avoid, areas such as narrow streets and routes where kidnappers can easily block you in.

the route is, however, the only way of accurately assessing any potential problem areas.

If Google does not automatically offer alternative route options for your intended journey, you can move the start and finish point of your route to a street nearby to your residence and office. Google will then plan alternative routes that will require only slight modifications to the start and end points. It is most important that you drive these alternative routes a number of times so you know them inside out and will become aware of any potential hazards and establish the viability of any escape paths. With a number of different routes open to you, the kidnappers will have a much harder time trying to guess which one you are going to take on any given occasion.

Alternatively, utilize a good SatNav. It can be programmed with different routes, and if you go off route to avoid a situation, it will automatically recalculate the route to your destination. This is by far the better option, although many SatNavs do not supply mapping data for high-risk areas in Asia, the Middle East, and the Far East.

It is essential that when you are reviewing possible alternative routes from and to your place of work you look for places where it is feasible for someone to stop you or block you in. Also be aware of things such as alleyways that allow for a potential blocking maneuver such as a vehicle pulling out in front of you.

When you are considering the route to be taken, two additional things have to be taken into consideration:

1. Where is the nearest police station and military base?
2. Where is there a place to lose anyone who might be following?

For example, nearly all airports have a large security and police presence. A drive into the short-term parking and then straight out again without paying will leave any pursuers with only two options:

1. Follow and be forced to stop and pay for the parking, or
2. Drive at high speed through the airport in an attempt to catch up to you.

If there is a possibility that you are being followed, this or a similar type of maneuver will force those following to reveal themselves and possibly dissuade them from continuing their surveillance.

In an extreme situation, it may be necessary for you to drive over a curb to escape your pursuers. This is not something you would wish to attempt under normal circumstances because of the potential for damaging the underside of the car, exhaust system, tires, or wheels. This is especially so in a normal sedan. In certain circumstances, it can, however, be a situation-changing tactic and at worst will result in a deflated tire and possibly a collapsed wheel. Although one or even two deflated tires may appear to totally incapacitate a car, even a moderately powerful sedan will be able to drive at a reasonable speed for many miles on the wheel rims alone.

There is a lot of science associated with the driving over curbs, but an attack angle into the curb of at least 25 degrees should be aimed for at the lowest speed practically possible. At an attack angle of less than 25 degrees, the wheel will simply skid off the curb with a substantial chance of breaking the tie joints, causing the wheel to fold under and leaving the car completely immobilized. Any angle of attack greater than 45 degrees will almost definitely deflate the tires and even collapse both wheels. This is especially so if the curb is approached at anything above a fast walking pace. Although two deflated tires are not necessarily an incapacitating condition for the car, collapsed wheels will be.

When depicted in the movies, a high-speed chase always looks good, with one car trying to outrun another or force it off the road. In real-life situations, this is, however, a bad decision to make. It is highly dangerous, and if the kidnappers are professional, they will have drivers who are far more adept at high-speed driving than any normal driver.

If you are being pursued, the key speeds at which to drive are over 20 mph (32 km/h) and under whatever you feel you can safely drive. For most people without special training, the upper limit will be in the region of 70–80 mph (112–129 km/h). Unless the car is traveling in a straight line, most people have little control over a vehicle traveling at 100 mph (160.9 km/h), and any sudden direction changes can result in the vehicle rolling over or skidding out of control and crashing.

It must not be forgotten that in any chase, there will be an effective speed difference of zero miles per hour between the chaser and the chased. Hence, it doesn't matter if you are driving at 50 mph (80.5 km/h) or 100 mph (160.9 km/h); the car behind will be doing exactly the same speed, and keeping the car there is a relatively simple job.

If the car is traveling no faster than 50 mph (80.5 km/h), then the speed can be increased or decreased, changing the effective speed of the following car by an appreciable amount. Another advantage of traveling at moderate speeds is if the following car pulls alongside, it is possible to turn into a side road, which will leave the chasing vehicle struggling to follow. At anything over 50 mph (80.5 km/h), such a maneuver for the chasing car would be close to impossible.

A recent development is the ability to purchase an in-car video recording unit. These are intended to record car accidents for insurance purposes. While they are designed to capture the view out of the front of the car, they can be used very effectively to capture an image of the car, its number plate, and the occupants of anyone following.

ADDITIONAL PRECAUTIONS

Avoid becoming boxed in by cars on either side when driving on a multi-lane highway. Always use the outside or inside lane instead of the middle lane. Such tactics can help you utilize routes of escape if you are attacked.

If you are ambushed, you should remember that the car can be used as both a shield and a weapon. If you are stopped in an ambush-type situation, it is best to stay in the vehicle with the doors locked. As soon as the situation permits, drive away as quickly as possible, even if it means using the vehicle to batter your way through any vehicles or other objects blocking your path.

You should always remember that if your life is in danger and there is no other way of escape, then you should have no compunction about driving through or over your attackers.

Learn to recognize and be alert to anything untoward that could be the start of an attempt to stop your car and kidnap you. Such events could include the following:

- A cyclist or motorcyclist falling in front of your car
- A workman stopping your car
- A road sign indicating an unusual detour
- A police or government checkpoint that does not seem quite right; however, be very careful in this type of situation, as it could be a real checkpoint, and if you run it, the police or military will almost certainly open fire
- Road blocked by a broken-down vehicle or accident victim
- An accident caused by another vehicle deliberately driving into yours
- Traffic that boxes you in unnecessarily
- Any sudden public demonstration or gunfire
- An unexplained absence of local people on the street

Any of these things or any combination of them could signal that a kidnap attempt is imminent.

If you conclude that you are about to become the victim of a kidnap, your decision as to what action to take will have to be instantaneous and without time to evaluate the consequences. You can, however, prepare yourself to make this decision by reviewing in your mind how best to react under a certain set of circumstances. This will mentally prepare you should such an incident occur. It is of absolutely no use after the event thinking, "If only I had taken that option, this would never have happened!"

Your options will be few, and picking the best solution will be difficult. Drawing attention to your car by sounding the horn is always a good starting point. If nothing else, this will ensure there will be witnesses to observe and report that you have been kidnapped.

If the situation permits, you could make a quick U-turn and try to escape. Driving through a vehicle blocking your path is, in extreme circumstances, an option, but this does come at some considerable risk to you and any passengers. If such an option is the only viable way out of a kidnap situation, always try to ensure that you hit the other vehicle with the impact focused on the corner of the vehicle you need to move out of the way, not sideways on a T impact. You should strive to make the impact at an angle, as this will be less likely to completely disable your car. The impact should also, if at all possible, be to the rear end of the vehicle, as this has less weight than the front, which contains the engine.

Any attempt to ram your way through the center of the vehicle or at an angle of 90° will only result in a huge accident, resulting in the car probably being completely immobilized. It must always be remembered that unless the attempt at driving through a stationary vehicle is conducted at a relatively slow speed, there is always the possibly of serious injury to you and your passengers.

Part of your preparation should include being comfortable with swerving into small spaces, blocking traffic, and sudden braking to assist your getaway. These skills can be perfected only by practice preferably under instruction from an experienced driver in such tactics. Many ex-Special Services personnel who work in high-risk areas are highly trained in such defensive driving skills and are generally available for such instruction.

If the circumstances allow the carrying of firearms, part of your anti-kidnapping training should include practicing the use of your weapon while driving. It would be of absolutely no use to have a weapon and not be able to shoot out tires or even the driver of another car without driving off the road or shooting innocent bystanders.

Make every attempt to improve your foreign language skills, as some ability to speak, read, and understand the local dialect could assist with threat assessment, communication with locals, and your ability to read and understand road signs while driving in unfamiliar terrain.

Ensure that at all times you have a clear 360° area of vision from your vehicle. Your ability to avoid threats requires a completely clear line of sight through all of the windows of your vehicle. Do not have hanging car fresheners, window stickers, toy animals on the rear parcel shelf, nodding dogs, or anything else that would in any way lead to a blind spot, no matter how small.

Avoid civil disturbances at all costs. Tear gas, gunfire, grenades, and rockets are not things one should go anywhere near. In countries where such civil disturbances are common, it will be necessary to learn how to effectively utilize bulletproof armor, retaining walls, and natural barriers to avoid damage to you and your vehicle should you be accidentally caught up in such a disturbance. The use of covert body armor should be a normal everyday precaution in any high-risk kidnap area.

Participate in professionally run courses to learn U-, J-, and bootlegger turns (see pp. 85–87), as well as effective ways to escape from vehicles that may prove a threat. These skills should be practiced time and time again until they are second nature. It is no use having to think about the techniques required to execute, for example, a J-turn when being followed at high speed by weapon-wielding kidnappers.

You and your vehicle and the way it is driven influence your vulnerability to terrorist kidnapping. Your first consideration must always be to lower your profile as a kidnap target. Use a plain, slightly less than pristine car that doesn't attract attention to you as being a "rich target." Avoid government cars, especially ones with diplomatic plates, that will immediately identify you as being an employee of the United States or other government. Large black SUVs with blacked out windows are an instant giveaway that you work for the U.S. government or one of its affiliates.

Any attempted kidnapping will almost always occur outside your home or office and after your habits and routes to and from work have been firmly established through extensive surveillance. The more precautions you take to reduce the predictability of your habits, the less likely it will be that you are going to become a selected target. The route taken between your home and place of work is the most easily predictable habit that can be utilized by a terrorist, and it is essential that you vary these routes and times of day that they are taken as much as possible.

Rendering yourself immune to a kidnap attempt is all but impossible. There are, however, numerous simple measures that you can place into operation to minimize the level of risk to you and your family. The following measures are very useful in high-threat areas but can be implemented no matter where your duties, work, or pleasure trips take you.

The practice of ensuring that you park at night in a well-lit and frequented area is of prime importance. Not only does the selection of area decrease the likelihood of your being kidnapped, but it also increases the level of general threat awareness for a driver. One should also avoid isolated parking spaces and spots situated close to a wall, blind alleyways, tall bushes, or large trees.

Before walking into a car parking area, assess your surroundings, pay attention to people who appear to be casually sitting in their vehicles, and look for a quick and easy exit route. If when walking to your car you are approached by a stranger, immediately change direction and head for a busy location. When approaching your vehicle, look under, around, and inside the car. An inspection mirror on a telescopic rod is ideal for checking under a vehicle.

Ensure that you have your vehicle keys in your hand and will not have to waste time searching through pockets, a briefcase, and so on. The keys also make for a convenient stabbing weapon should the situation arise.

If you need to load anything into your car, make sure that you do not turn your back on the car park. In a high-threat situation, it will always be preferable to put the packages on the rear seat rather than in the trunk.

When you feel that there are no immediate threats, open the door, enter quickly, lock the doors, and ensure the windows are fully closed. Lingering in a car park will only increase your susceptibility as a target for kidnappers, so start the car as soon as possible and drive quickly away.

There are those infrequent occasions when a kidnapper will force the victim to drive the car. If such a situation occurs, it is essential to ensure that you put on your seat belt and at the first opportunity crash the car into some stationary object. Deliberately crashing the car at a busy junction or traffic light will immediately bring rescuers and the police to the scene.

This is not such a dangerous tactic as it seems at first glance. The driver would have already have the seat belt tightly fastened and have had the opportunity of bracing him- or herself against the impact. In addition, the kidnapper will almost certainly not have fastened the seat belt, which could result in him receiving an incapacitating injury during the crash.

TACTICAL DRIVING

Tactical driving covers both defensive driving (which involves no contact with another car) and offensive driving (which can include contact with another car or object) and is one of the skills necessary to effectively guard against vehicular ambushes.

Anyone, and especially those in high-risk areas, may be considered as a potential target for being kidnapped. It is essential that everyone traveling or who is a resident in a high-threat area has a basic understanding of the techniques and skills of tactical driving. It is, however, of absolutely no use if the knowledge is only possessed. These skills must be practiced in a safe environment until they become second nature.

Defensive driving includes fundamentals of safe driving, tactical driving, pursuit driving, response driving, evasive driving, and others. Defensive driving is a style of driving using specific skills and techniques to accomplish a specific outcome. There are many courses available that purport to teach these skills, although these courses do vary very much in the quality of instruction.

A typical safe driving course would also teach a driver to check things such as tire pressure, oil, water, fuel, and battery. These kinds of lessons are more related to safe driving in general rather than defensive driving, but they can be critical nonetheless. For example, checking that there is sufficient engine oil is vital to prevent the engine from seizing if the level is low but would not necessarily assist you in being able to drive yourself out of a high-risk situation.

THREE BASIC RULES OF DEFENSIVE DRIVING

The first rule is to ensure that the front and rear of the vehicle are protected. This is called the "two-second rule." This rule is useful, as it is independent of the vehicle's speed and equates to one vehicle length for every 5 mph (8 km/h) of the vehicle's speed. At 5 mph (8 km/h), two seconds will equate to one vehicle length; at 50 mph (88 km/h), it equates to ten vehicle lengths; and so on. Allowance of additional seconds must be added to allow for abnormal environmental conditions, that is, snow, ice, and heavy standing water.

The second rule states that a safe space must be maintained at the sides of the vehicle. This is called the "doors-width rule," and basically it translates to having at least the width of a door between you and any adjacent vehicle. If you are traveling down the center of a three-lane road, then the door width would apply on either side of your car. As with the two-second rule, as the speed increases so should the separating distance to allow for reaction time.

The third rule is called the "diagonal rule" (see Figure 5.2). This states that when you are traveling in a multilane system at a similar speed to other traffic, you should always position the vehicle *diagonally* to other vehicles. That is, do not travel alongside another vehicle, which may steer toward you, as you may come into contact.

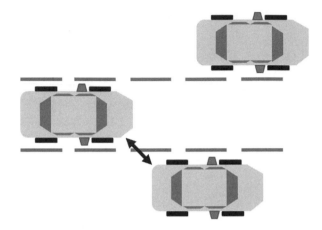

Figure 5.2   An illustration of the diagonal rule.

USING THE VEHICLE AS A BATTERING RAM

If the vehicle is front wheel drive, as many are nowadays, you should avoid at all costs driving into a suspect vehicle. Such an impact in a front wheel drive car will probably destroy the radiator, engine, and steering. If such a tactic is necessary when driving a front wheel drive car, then the rear of the car makes a far more reasonable battering ram. If you take this option, the trunk will take the impact rather than the radiator, engine, and relatively delicate constant velocity joints. As reverse gear has a much lower ratio than most of the forward gears, any speed generated will probably be lower than when going forward.

A problem with victims using the vehicle as a battering ram to drive their way out of a situation is that even in a life-and-death situation, people are reluctant to damage their car. You must overcome that feeling, and if the situation calls for it, hit the other car or any other object blocking your way as hard as possible.

You must always remember that after you have taken such an action, it is essential for the car to still be in a drivable condition. The key in this situation is that once you have rammed the other car, move away from the danger as fast as possible, as the occupants of the other car will likely be in shock and will take some time to recover. If your car is undrivable, the occupants of the other car can recover and are likely to be very upset at your actions. Hanging around is therefore not an option!

GENERAL TIPS FOR DRIVING AWARENESS AND SAFETY

Sounding the horn is always a good strategy, as this will bring attention to the suspected kidnappers, which is never a good option as far as they are concerned. Other quick tips include keeping the windows up and ensuring that at all times the gas tank is at least a quarter full.

If you feel something is not right, use your mobile phone to call someone and explain your situation. If you cannot reach anyone, leave a voice or text message on your voice mail, with a description of your location and where you are going.

If you are kidnapped, keep your phone with you and switched on with the sound muted. The police will be able to track its whereabouts and find you. Your kidnappers will be aware of this facility, so make all attempts to hide it from them.

Tactical, defensive, and offensive driving are like any other skills; they take practice. Your life may well depend on these skills. They must, therefore, be practiced until they become second nature and do not require conscious thought.

SPECIALIZED DRIVING TECHNIQUES

Another important driving skill is the ability to perform a quick maneuver to change the direction in which your car is traveling. This type of turn is especially important if your vehicle is going in reverse. The method of accomplishing this is called the J-turn, and the end product is to have the vehicle maintain its course but turn through 180°. Another specialized technique is called the "bootleggers turn." This is essentially the same as the J-turn but carried out while the vehicle is moving in a forward direction. A handbrake turn is another method of changing the vehicle's direction by 180° so that the vehicle completely reverses its direction of travel.

J-Turn

The J-turn is a method of rapidly changing direction by 180°, starting in reverse and ending up pointing forward. This is predominantly an evasive driving maneuver and is extremely effective when kidnap appears imminent. When you are first attempting to learn and perfect this technique, it is better to start with low-grip surfaces such as wet tarmac or, even better, a grassy field. Also ensure that there aren't any nearby obstacles such as lampposts, trees, or brick walls in the immediate vicinity. Once you're confident, you can attempt the maneuver on dry tarmac, but this type of surface will require higher speeds, which could well result in things going wrong much faster.

First, turn off the car's electronic stability program, put the car in reverse gear, and make sure that you are looking over your shoulder and out of the rear window. Accelerate to between 17 and 20 mph (27 and 32 km/h). At any speed less than this, there is a likelihood of rolling the car, as the tires will be gripping the road rather than sliding. When you're ready to execute the turn, depress the clutch, brake very hard, and spin the steering wheel at least one complete turn. Be violent with the steering wheel, as you need to get the car sliding into the turn. As the car starts turning and the turn is approaching 90° to your starting point, begin straightening up the steering wheel, but not completely. Quickly engage second gear (never first, as this will lead to an uncontrollable skid) and release the clutch as soon as you are facing in the correct direction. If you release the clutch before you are facing the direction in which you want to finally end up going, the car will continue to spin out of control. As soon as the car is stable, accelerate hard and move off in a forward direction.

If you are having problems getting the front end of the car around, increase the speed slightly or apply a quick flick of the steering wheel in the opposite direction to unsettle the car. This flicking of the steering wheel in the opposite direction mid-maneuver is called a "reverse Scandinavian flick."

Bootleggers Turn

This type of turn takes its name from the U.S. bootleggers who transported illegal liquor to their customers during the Prohibition era using highly modified cars and spectacular driving techniques, including the bootleggers turn, to escape authorities.

A bootleggers turn is a driving maneuver to reverse the direction of travel of a forward-moving vehicle (not as in a J-turn when the vehicle starts by traveling backward) by 180° and still stay within the width of a two-lane road. The bootleggers turn is also known as a "smuggler's turn" or power slide and is essentially a forward-facing version of the J-turn. The technique is, however, quite dissimilar.

While you are traveling in a forward direction, quickly drop down into a lower gear, preferably second, and then with some violence turn the steering wheel toward the opposite lane. The car should then begin a controlled skid across the road to the opposite lane. If the turn is correctly executed, the car will come to a full stop, pointing in the opposite direction. First gear can then be selected, the accelerator floored, and the clutch dropped to accelerate away in the opposite direction.

As with the J-turn, an initial flick of the steering wheel the wrong way will assist in transferring the load to the outer wheels. This will start the car moving into a skid before you finally turn the wheel in the direction you want to end up.

Cars with automatic transmissions are incapable of performing this maneuver, as the wheels must be made to spin to aid the turn. It is also very difficult to perform this turn in a front wheel drive car. Cars with automatic transmissions can be modified to make the turn possible, but this is quite a complex undertaking. Such a modification is often used by stunt drivers in films, as the automatic transmission gives the driver one less thing to have to think about.

Handbrake Turn

A handbrake turn is another method of turning the car through 180° without using a bootleggers turn. If you are driving very fast, you can also use it to quickly negotiate tight corners. Essentially a handbrake turn is the same as a bootleggers turn but you use the handbrake instead of spinning the rear tires to initiate the turn.

Start by violently turning the steering wheel in the opposite direction you want to go, thus transferring the car's weight to the outside tires. Then pull on the handbrake as hard and fast as possible, which will cause the rear wheels to lock and lose adhesion with the road. With the steering wheels turned, the rear of the car begins to slide around in the direction required. As soon as the car attains the correct position in the opposite lane, release the handbrake, and you can accelerate the vehicle away in the opposite direction.

As with the J-turn and bootleggers turn, the handbrake turn does, if the speed is too low, pose a serious risk of the car rolling over. SUVs and high-sided vehicles are more prone than sedans or sports cars to this.

Guardrails, trees, or other vehicles can pose a distinct hazard when you are performing these maneuvers, and you should be very much aware of your surroundings before attempting these turns. Likewise going too fast or even too slow will result in the vehicle spinning off the road rather than rotating.

With any of these techniques, releasing the handbrake too soon while the car is still sliding sideways will also cause the car to drive off the road.

As with all defensive driving skills, you must practice these turns time and time again until they become second nature. Damp grass or wet tarmac will make the initial attempts much easier to perform, and from there you can progress to dry tarmac and concrete surfaces.

SOURCES

Driving Standards Agency, *Driving: The Essential Skills; Safe Driving for Life* (Stationery Office Books, 2001).

Philip Coyne and Penny Mares, *Roadcraft: The Police Driver's Handbook* (The Police Foundation, 2013).

Richard Alan Heene, *Offensive Driving* (Dick Weenie Productions, 1995).

Driving Standards Agency, *The Official DSA Guide to Driving: The Essential Skills* (Stationery Office Books, 2010).

DDT Group, Driver Training, Defensive Driving, Advanced Driving, www.ddt-group.com/.

"Top 10 Safe Driving Tips," GE Capital, www.gecapital.co.uk/en/docs/GE_Capital_Safe_Driving_Top_Tips.pdf.

"Defensive Driving Tips," North Star Driving School, northstardrivingsch.tripod.com/id50.htm.

"How to Drive Tactically (Technical Driving)," http://www.wikihow.com/Drive-Tactically-%28Technical-Driving%29.

CRI Counter Terrorism and Israeli Tactical Driving, Offensive, www.critraining.com/.

"Driving Techniques for Escape and Evasion," www.angelfire.com/clone2/dark-corner/evasive.html.

"Evasive Driving Moves!" full-contact.military.com.

"Evasive Driving Techniques," LowProfileLiving.com.

"Evasive and Offensive Driving Techniques: Training Days," http://www.close-protectionworld.com/driving-forum/74342-evasive-offensive-driving-tech-niques-training-days.html.

"Defensive Driving Overseas," U.S. Department of Agriculture, http://www.dm.usda.gov/ocpm/Security%20Guide/T5terror/Driving.htm.

6

Self-Defense Strategies

Most people have no idea how to defend themselves against even the most amateurish mugger let alone a well-organized and determined kidnapper. Unfortunately, people tend to think that what they see in films and TV programs can be achieved by the average man on the street. An organized kidnapper armed or otherwise will nearly always have the element of surprise on his side, and the victim will be overpowered in a matter of seconds. Even a person experienced in martial arts will have little chance against a surprise attack by an armed assailant.

There are basic survival instincts with which we are born that are wired into our brains and are intended to keep us alive. These reactions are instinctive and are invoked when we are placed in a dangerous situation. When one's automatic responses to a specific threat are called forth, the odds of emerging as a survivor from that threat rise dramatically.

SELF-DEFENSE CONCEPTS

For you to survive an armed attack that could lead to a kidnapping, there are three self-defense concepts in which you must be become proficient:

1. Catch
2. Control
3. Neutralize

Catch

The first step in surviving an armed kidnap attempt is to restrain the arm that has the weapon. It does not matter if the attacker has a revolver, self-loading pistol, club, or knife; if the attacker cannot utilize the weapon effectively against you, he cannot injure or subdue you with it.

As the arm presents a much larger target and thus moves much slower than the hand, restraining it is going to be much easier than trying to restrain the hand.

Control

The second step to surviving an abduction attempt is to immediately control the weapon after you have restrained the arm holding the weapon. There are some robust techniques for developing the skills necessary to effectively control a weapon, and they are not at all complicated or difficult to learn and practice.

The first thing to remember is to hold on to the suspect's weapon as if your life and liberty depend on it, because they do. The most basic exercise to develop your proficiency in controlling your abductor's weapon is to have an assistant hold a marker pen and try to write on you while you attempt to prevent him from doing so. This sounds very simple, but it provides the most basic of skills that might save your life. *Practice* is the all-important word here, as the more you practice, the more instinctive the action will become.

With regard to the weapon held by your abductor, it will always be much easier to safely control a gun or blunt instrument than a bladed weapon. An abductor must be able to strike you with a blunt instrument to inflict damage, and this requires some space in which to swing the weapon. If the abductor has a firearm, he must be able to point it at you if he has any chance of shooting you. A bladed weapon, however, can be used to slash or stab from close in or at arm's length. If you fight for control of a bladed weapon, you must, therefore, expect to be cut. It is essential that you mentally prepare yourself to deal with the pain and shock of being cut or stabbed and the sight of your own blood.

Neutralize

The final step in surviving an assault with a weapon is to ensure that your attacker has been effectively neutralized.

Once you have restrained the attacker's weapon and have control of it, you must ensure that the abductor is rendered completely incapable of taking further action against you. Sometimes it may be necessary to use the suspect's weapon to put an end to the attack and place the attacker out of action. If you are forced into this situation, you must ignore any moral and legal responsibilities that may exist and ensure that your attacker is permanently disabled and not merely deprived of the weapon.

It is important to practice neutralizing an attacker and ensure that it becomes second nature. It is of absolutely no use to mentally go through a checklist once your freedom has been compromised. You must begin this mental preparation by arming a training partner with a toy gun, rubber knife, or marker pen and start from a position where your partner is controlling the training aid. Practice using various scenarios until neutralizing an attacker becomes second nature. Never forget that butting the head, gouging the eyes, or kneeing the groin are simple and highly effective ways of neutralizing an attacker. It is not possible to overstate the importance of repeatedly practicing these skills until they become second nature.

UNIVERSAL FLINCH THEORY

There is a concept called the "universal flinch theory" which contends that everyone naturally flinches in exactly the same way relative to their sentience and immediacy to a threat.[1] This flinch reaction is independent of age, gender, or size and is inbuilt into our brains as an automatic survival reflex reaction. It is this survival reflex that combat specialists have studied and concluded that by subconsciously recognizing this instinct, one can better protect oneself against attack. Commercial companies run courses on how to stimulate this survival reflex response by ensuring that the autoresponse part of the brain acts to provide a self-protective and automatic action.

During a sudden, aggressive attack, the perceptive part of the brain cannot process the mode of attack and would normally freeze. Instead, the autoresponse mechanism overrides this response, producing a flinch. The idea is to convert this primal survival flinch response into a self-survival tactic by tapping into this autosurvival memory and accessing the deeply routed reflexes that have kept man alive.

STRATEGIES FOR SELF-PROTECTION

Irrespective of the type of training, if the abductor is about to strike, it is now your fight. And there may be professional rules of engagement for use by soldiers and combatants in a sporting environment, this is now a very personal moment. If you can't overcome this threat, then the outcome is predictable: you will be kidnapped and possibly seriously injured or even killed.

Do whatever is necessary, no matter how violent it may be, to get away; this isn't a boxing match with Queensbury rules and regulations. Pick up and employ any heavy object that is close at hand: a brick, piece of piping, or large piece of wood. Whatever the object you manage to find, use it with the greatest force that you can marshal and use it repeatedly until your assailant is totally incapacitated.

If you have tear gas, a stun gun, a knife, or an edged weapon, use it. If you can legally carry one or more of these defensive weapons, practice with them. A weapon forgotten in a purse or briefcase is useless; it must be instantly available and ready to be used and used effectively.

Don't feel safe just because you have Mace or pepper spray on you. If you are not completely familiar with how your weapon works and have to spend time trying to figure out how to take the safety off, it merely gives your attacker a handy weapon to use against you. It must always be at hand with the safety catch off and ready to use. Scrabbling around in the dark trying to locate and disengage the safety will lose you those vital seconds that may make the difference between capture and freedom.

If you have a rape alarm, always have it at hand with the operating cord permanently attached to your wrist. Once again, it is of absolutely no use to have it hidden away in a pocket, handbag, or briefcase. It must be instantly available.

If you have a firearm, always have it ready and in either a shoulder holster or a belt holster. An ankle holster is of little use, as it may be inaccessible in time of crisis, as is having it tucked into your trouser top. A firearm stuck in the top of your trousers is likely to catch on the belt and, once again, will lose you vital seconds as you attempt to disentangle it.

Practice time and time again getting the weapon out of the holster and pointed in the right direction in a cocked and ready-to-fire position. Do not use a holster with a safety strap; it will simply result in wasted seconds as you unfasten it.

With a self-loading weapon, never keep it in the holster without a round in the chamber. You will waste valuable time pulling back the slide to chamber a round, to say nothing of the possibility of not chambering a round correctly if you are panicking. If a round is in the chamber, all that is necessary is to cock the hammer to make it ready to fire.

Modern revolvers do not need to be kept with an empty chamber under the hammer, as modern safeties are all but infallible. Always keep the weapon loaded with a full complement of ammunition. It is unwise, however, to keep a revolver cocked when in the holster, as you can inadvertently pull the trigger when drawing the weapon.

If an abductor attempts to grab hold of you, don't be troubled over using your teeth. When biting, always try to bite with the front of your teeth. Do not take a huge bite but rather take a "pinch" of skin, as this will cause far more damage and pain than a full mouth bite. It will be easier to bite off part of an ear, nose, or finger in this way. Using your teeth in this way will provide you with the valuable seconds you need to escape.

When punching or kicking, aim for sensitive spots. Stick your fingers in the eyes and hit, kick, or knee the groin, nose, throat, or kidneys. Scrape your foot down the shin, and use your heel to stomp on the top of the attacker's foot or kick sideways into his knee. Both techniques will cause considerable pain and possibly even permanent damage.

Your knees and elbows and the heel of your hand are all good striking weapons, and although your closed fist can be used with great effect as a hammer, *don't throw punches.* You are more likely to break the thin bones in your hand or wrist and put yourself out of action than to seriously hurt your attacker.

Ensure that each and every strike makes contact and is landed with the greatest force possible and that each one counts. Do not, under any circumstances, stop. Continue your attack until there is no further chance of the attacker having the ability to continue the attack. One good blow is not enough, as it will probably merely hurt your attacker and make him extremely angry. The idea is to completely stop the assault and ensure that there is absolutely no chance of it continuing. Such a drastic step may require that you inflict a life-threatening amount of damage to your abductor, but that is not your immediate concern. At this juncture, the only thing that should concern you is escaping safely.

Keep striking out as hard and as frequently as possible until the abductor ceases to move. Do not have any misgivings about using this degree of violence; it is your freedom and possibly your life that you are fighting for.

Your primary aim is not to kill the opponent, just to stop the abduction. If the attacker dies, then this is merely collateral damage and a side effect of stopping the attack. Any moral or legal concerns can be dealt with at a later date once you are free and have reached a safe haven.

93

Do not flail your arms around or strike out with your nails, as these are totally ineffective self-defense techniques. The flailing of your arms and scratching with your nails will only cause defensive marks on the attacker's face and arms and will only provide forensic evidence on your dead body.

Once you are out of the hold, run as fast as you can and get as far away from your attacker as possible. Then, and only then, call the appropriate police emergency number. Always ensure that you have this as your number-one speed dial.

If you cannot get away from your attacker, then try to delay him, for example, by locking yourself in a room. This may give the police time to reach you and arrest the abductor. If, however, you are kidnapped, attempt to conceal your mobile phone and call the police when your captor isn't looking. If you don't have a mobile phone, use any landline phone that may be available. If it is a pay phone, calls to emergency numbers from these are, in most countries, usually free.

If you have managed to thwart the abductor and he runs away, get to a nearby house or business as quickly as possible and let people know what happened and have them call the police.

This will then

1. Place you in a safe environment
2. Alert the police
3. Create witnesses

Previous advice has always been to cooperate with your attackers, as there is less likelihood of your getting hurt. However, recent experiences have shown that the old advice simply isn't true. Now the advice is, "The quicker you respond to the attack and escape, the more likely you are to survive the encounter."

In the first few seconds, confusion abounds on both sides, as the kidnappers have no idea how you're going to respond. At this juncture, you will have far more options open to you, and making the best use of this period of confusion is crucial if you are going to escape.

Some safety precautions include the following:

- Always be aware of your surroundings and who is nearby when you are in a public place.
- Do not play loud music or even wear headphones, as it isolates you from your surroundings.
- Every time you enter a new environment, make it a habit to spot and plan escape routes.

- Avoid dark alleys and parking areas.
- Always carry a mobile phone with a local SIM card.
- Always make sure your mobile phone is fully charged.
- Always carry some type of safety device such as a loud personal (rape) alarm or a self-defense weapon.
- When overseas, always carry a local paper or magazine. This will make you less noticeable.
- Arrange for taxis through your hotel front desk. Don't pick one up on the street.
- Read the travel advice given on the U.S. Department of State website or the foreign office website or through your travel agent.
- If you get a bad feeling about someone or the area you are in, listen to your instincts no matter how irrational they seem.
- Walking into a store, changing the direction of your travel, and staying with others are all good examples of how you can spot someone tailing you and avoid being kidnapped.
- An abductor will always have the upper hand, as he would have planned in advance and have the element of surprise over you. You must, therefore, always make a plan of escape well in advance.

It is possible for you to prepare yourself by advance evaluation of your situation by doing the following:

- Anticipate the method and location of any kidnap attempt you are likely to encounter.
- Predict your likely reaction when the kidnap attempt is made.
- Rehearse the possible kidnap scenarios and their outcomes in your mind. This will preempt your likely response and enable you to act instantly should you be attacked.

Be prepared to resist by doing the following:

- Carry Mace or pepper spray (see Figure 6.1).
- Carry a steel extendible baton.
- Use your keys to rake across the attacker's eyes.
- Hold a key between your fingers as a stabbing weapon. This will probably damage the tendons in your own hand, but it will do far more damage to the attacker.
- Apply for and carry a small firearm if you believe your risk level is high and the local legislation allows.

Figure 6.1 Pepper spray can be a useful tool against a would-be kidnapper.

If there are more than two armed kidnappers involved in an attempted attack, there is, plausibly, little or no chance of escape. In such a scenario, you should, despite what has been said before, be compliant from the very commencement of the attack. Statistics show that when more than two abductors has committed the kidnap and the victim has cooperated, approximately 95 percent of victims are released alive.

These statistics also show that under such circumstances, the chance of being killed is greatest during the first few minutes of an abduction. Whether this is due to the kidnapper being in a heightened state of agitation when in close proximity to other armed kidnappers is unclear. In such circumstances, it is, therefore, imperative to cooperate from the very beginning.

However, if there are two or fewer unarmed kidnappers, you are in the vicinity of other people, and you can quickly get help, then you should fight and do everything possible to escape. Once you have made the decision to escape, make every attempt to reach a safe place and continue to shout as loudly as you can for help. Whatever you do, don't look back, as it will only slow your progress, and don't stop running until you've reached safety.

What qualifies as safety depends on the exact circumstances, and each one will be different. However, drawing the attention of police officers or the military will generally be sufficient and will probably bring in a crowd of people as well.

However, being in a crowd or close to the police or military will help only if you ensure that those around you know exactly what the threat to your safety is. As mentioned earlier, it is essential that you shout out as loudly as you can that you are being kidnapped and, if possible, include a description of those who are attempting to abduct you.

If you are in a kidnap hotspot in a country hostile to foreigners and especially if it is rife with corruption, it will often be the case that the police cannot be fully trusted and that safety will be attained only once you are within your embassy.

If you become too tired to continue running, then make a scene. Shout at the top of your voice or blow a whistle; in fact do anything that will bring attention to yourself and your abductor. Shouting "FIRE!" at the top of your lungs will attract passersby, and although it may be against local laws, your liberty and possibly even your life are at stake. The fire scenario is especially effective in or near a public building where the abductor hopes to remain inconspicuous. Drawing attention to yourself and the abductor will, hopefully, draw crowds toward you and bring unwanted attention to the abductor and, hopefully, cause him to flee the scene.

While it may not be appropriate in Islamic countries, grabbing on to people will make it difficult for a potential abductee to drag you away. Grab hold of a bystander and hold on with all your might while screaming and explaining the situation. The bystander will now be involved in a fight against the abductor, and having another person involved will shift the odds in your favor. Such a tactic is especially effective if you are a woman or child. If there aren't any people around, hold on to something large, such as a lamppost, parking meter, or bicycle. A bicycle also makes a good weapon if thrown at the abductor, as the frame, wheel spokes, and pedals will tangle up the abductor.

Even if you can't get away from an abductor using any of the foregoing, you can try to make it as difficult as possible for him to take you away against your will. In addition, the commotion caused will almost certainly draw a crowd of people who can act as witnesses to the kidnap.

When children are the target of a kidnapper, the situation is quite different, as they are less able to either defend themselves or run away with any realistic chance of escape. In such instances, the involvement of others is usually the only chance of escape. Children must be taught not to simply scream for help, as people are generally inclined to ignore such a plea. If possible children should shout out that they are being kidnapped and try to convey to anyone around a description of the kidnapper. This should discourage the kidnapper or, at the very least, convince any bystanders that the kidnap attempt is real and not a game. If the child is unable to escape and is kidnapped, it will, at the very least, leave a dependable picture for the police to work from.

A self-defense course should be mandatory for anyone traveling in a high-risk area; however, specialized knowledge is generally unnecessary to thwart an attack. You also do not have to win a fight with an attacker to successfully escape. The only reason to fight with your attacker is to elude his grip and if necessary disable him and escape as fast as possible. Put up enough resistance, and the kidnapper may consider that you are going to be too much trouble to deal with and give up.

It must always be remembered that this is not a structured fight with regulations and rules of engagement. You should fight as dirty as you can and with absolutely no holds barred! Absolutely anything goes in your attempt to get away, as there are no Queensbury or other rules of engagement.

If a heavy object is close at hand, such as a rock, metal pole, large piece of wood, and so on, use it with as much force as you can muster. If you have tear gas spray or a stun gun, do not hold back fearing the consequences. Use the gas by firing it straight into the attacker's eyes. Use your car keys to rake across the attacker's face or stab into his eyes. Make use of your teeth to bite off part of an ear, finger, or nose. Your forehead and elbows and the heel of your hand can be used to crush the nasal bone. Crushing the nasal bone in this way is especially effective, as it produces exceptional pain, and the associated reflex action closes the eyes, which will give you additional time to escape.

Make each and every strike count, but on no account stand up and fight, but run the instant the abductor is fully out of commission. Do not, under any circumstances, stand around to see if he is going to recover. Run as fast and as far away as you can as soon as you can.

If a kidnapper attempts to grab you, swing your arms wildly. Swinging and waving your arms around will make it difficult for at attacker to obtain and keep hold of you. This is referred to as the "windmill effect." Windmilling is simply a way of making it extremely difficult for an abductor to get hold of you. However, as mentioned earlier, do not flail your arms about wildly as a form of attack, as this will have little or no effect on an abductor.

You should do anything you can think of to make the abductor feel that he is being watched or that there are circumstances beyond his control that could have a negative outcome for him. This will probably involve you in a considerable amount of lying about things that don't exist. For example,

- Say, "I am suffering from chronic effervescing pneumonia [a non-existent disease], and I have to take my medicine three times a day or I'll die. If I don't take my medicine, then you will be looking at a murder charge."
- Point to anything that even remotely looks like a camera and tell the kidnapper that he is under surveillance.
- Point to an ATM and tell the abductor that it has a camera and he is in full view and being videoed.
- Even if you have not had an opportunity to phone the police on your mobile, tell the abductor that you have pressed the speed dial button and that the police are on their way.
- If you think people are following you, turn around to face them and stare directly at their face. They will then know with certainty that you have seen their face and you could either pick them out from mug shots or create a police Photofit. Such tactics could be enough to dissuade the abductors from proceeding further.
- If the abductor is carrying a weapon, focus deliberately on his face, not the weapon. It is natural for you to keep your eyes on the weapon, fearing that it may be fired or used to stab you, but this detracts from memorizing what the attacker looks like. Your attention must be maintained on the attacker's face so that afterward you are able to relate the attacker's description to the police.
- Even if the attacker has a gun, running away is not an option you should discard. Obtaining a ransom is normally the abductor's only consideration, and he doesn't want you dead, at least not before he has received the money. If other people are in the vicinity, it is most unlikely that the attacker will open fire anyway. The last thing the abductor will want is for the crowd to turn hostile because he has shot an innocent bystander. In addition, unless the abductor is a trained marksman, the likelihood of him hitting a target that is running away in a zigzag fashion is highly unlikely. The greater the distance you can place between yourself and the attacker, the less likely it will be that he will even attempt a shot.

ABDUCTION BY CAR

- If an abductor is trying to force you into a car, it is essential that you do absolutely everything possible to stay outside of it. Once you are inside a car, your chance of escape is dramatically reduced.
- Using your arms and legs to jam yourself in the car's doorway will make it extremely difficult for even two people to force you inside.
- If at all possible, keep your head outside and above the car. Not only does it make it far more difficult to push you in, but you will be able to scream and attract passersby far more effectively with your head outside.
- If you're forced into a vehicle, slide across the seat, open the door on the other side, and get out.
- If you are forced into the vehicle and cannot get out, try to jam something into the ignition lock before the abductor inserts the key into the ignition. Jam a nail file, a piece of metal such as a nail, a toothpick, the chewing gum in your mouth, or even your own car keys in the ignition lock. Any of these will effectively prevent the kidnapper from inserting the car key and starting the vehicle.
- If the keys are already in the ignition lock and the engine is not running, break the key off in the lock. This is quite easy to do and will completely immobilize the car. If the ignition is switched on and the engine is already running, pull the keys out and throw them out of the window as far as you can.

If you are forced into the trunk, all is not lost, as it is still possible to escape. If you can't get out by kicking open the trunk lid, kick out the panel leading to the rear light cluster and disable or punch out the lights. Sticking your arm out through the hole will alert other motorists that you are trapped inside the trunk.

If you are unable to knock the lights out, disconnect the wires, rendering the lights inoperative and possibly shorting out the whole of the car's electrics, stopping it dead. If you cannot do this, a disabled set of rear lights might just attract the attention of the police.

If none of these work, then every time the car stops, shout out as loud as you can and pound on the trunk lid. This will attract attention and hopefully bring the police.

Most of the cars produced over the past few years come with an emergency trunk release lever inside the trunk. If the kidnappers have not disabled this, you can pull the lever to open the trunk and when the car next slows down or stops make your escape.

It is also possible to open the trunk lock from inside the car, but this does take practice, especially when working in the dark and requires, at the very least, a Swiss Army knife. It is worth familiarizing yourself with the trunk-locking mechanism and how it can be opened from inside.

RESTRAINTS

At all costs avoid having your hands and legs restrained. Once you have been handcuffed or restrained with tape, cable ties, or rope, there is going to be little chance for escape. If you going to fight and/or run away, you must do it as soon as the kidnap attempt starts. Once you have been restrained, the kidnap is over, and there will be little or no chance of escape. You will not get a second chance.

BE OBSERVANT

If an abduction attempt has been made and you have escaped, make sure that you commit to memory as many details about your attacker as possible. You will then be able to relay the information to police, which will assist in the criminal's apprehension.

If you are in a country where the language is not your own, try to learn as many key phrases in the local language as possible. Not only will these phrases assist in your escape or evasion attempts, but you might also pick up additional information about the abductors. The local population will be more sympathetic to anyone who has taken the effort to learn some of their language, and they will also be more inclined to assist in your escape attempts.

It must not be forgotten, that if you cannot be understood, you cannot be helped!

ESCAPE AND RECAPTURE

Remember, if your escape attempt is unsuccessful, your abductors will be especially alert, and you will almost certainly not get another chance to escape. A severe beating will most likely be your reward for an unsuccessful escape attempt, so make sure that your first and, probably only, escape attempt is successful.

Your attacker will probably be somewhat more than angry if you fight back and attempt to escape. This anger will be exacerbated in direct proportion to any injury you may cause him and will result in beatings.

While some would-be abductors will give up when you fight back, many will continue to pursue you, especially if you have injured them. Do not restrain yourself when fighting back: be as vicious and use as much force as you possibly can.

DEALING WITH AN ABDUCTOR'S WEAPON

At this point it should be noted that there are numerous self-defense companies that specialize in teaching techniques for the disarming of an armed assailant. Some are excellent, but many are of dubious worth, and you should be very circumspect before signing up for such a course.

Self-defense weapons are dealt with in more detail in Chapter 9, but a brief description of how to defend yourself against a firearm, tear gas spray, or stun gun follows.

Self-Loading Pistol or Revolver

Not only is having a handgun pointed at you extremely unsettling, but it also has the potential to be a life-threatening experience (see Figure 6.2). Any attempt to disarm an abductor will place you in a life-threatening situation and should not be attempted unless there are no other options open to you.

Basics

For a firearm to discharge, the firing pin has to fall onto the primer of the cartridge. Many weapons have an exposed hammer, and although placing your hand over the top of the weapon, thus stopping the hammer from falling, is often proposed, this is an extremely dangerous strategy.

This dubious technique, for obvious reasons, does not work on a hammerless weapon, and even if the weapon in question does have an exposed hammer, the assailant simply has to pull the weapon away from the victim to place the weapon back in working order. It is also likely that

102

Figure 6.2 Having a handgun pointed directly at you is unnerving and clearly life threatening. Thus, do not attempt to disarm an abductor in such situations unless there is no other option.

the trigger will have been inadvertently pulled during your attempt to disable the weapon, and at this point your hand is the only thing stopping the hammer from dropping. Under such conditions, once the gun has been pulled away from your hand, the hammer will automatically drop, firing the weapon. This will almost certainly result in a serious or fatal gunshot wound to you.

Disarming an Armed Assailant

There are numerous methods listed for disarming an assailant, some of which are downright dangerous, others that are completely useless, and some that are so complicated they are all but impossible to fathom.

However, those techniques that are practical and relatively safe all follow the same basic principles. They can also be applied whether the weapon is being held in one or both hands.

1. First, grab the rear of the gun, making sure that neither hand covers the muzzle, preferably with one hand over the top and one coming from underneath.
2. Twist the gun away from your body and in an upward direction.

3. Using the gun as a lever, apply as much rotational pressure away from you as possible. With luck this will break the assailant's trigger finger and, if sufficient force is used, possibly the wrist as well.
4. It is possible that the gun will fire during this maneuver, but at this point the weapon will be pointing away from you, and a discharge should be relatively safe.
5. Once the gun is pointing well away from you, step in and deliver a knee to the groin, slide the instep of your shoe down the shin, or stamp on the abductor's foot. If you are close enough and have your back to the assailant, you can jerk your head back into the assailant's face, smashing his nasal bone.
6. Once the assailant has been disarmed by this technique, you can use the gun to hold him until help arrives or, if he has another weapon and tries to use it on you, shoot him (hopefully not fatally!).

This and the many other effective methods of disarming an attacker require training to the extent that the actions become instinctive. If you find yourself in an armed abduction situation, it is no use to mentally have to go through the disarming steps one by one. It has to be so ingrained in the memory that it happens automatically.

Timing the Disarming

The timing of the disarming is extremely important. When an attacker first approaches his victim, he has only one thing on his mind and that is to threaten the victim into submission with the weapon. He is also likely to be on an adrenaline high and to be highly unstable. At this stage any attempt at disarming him could result in your being shot, possibly fatally.

You should wait until the abductor has calmed down and his brain has to envisage other actions, such as directing you to a car or indicating that you should move in a certain direction. If he can be made to give verbal directions as well, all the better, as this will give him even more things for his brain to compute.

It is at this juncture that any attempt at disarming him should be made, as his brain is dealing with several matters at one time and cannot concentrate on the gun and trigger finger alone. Not only that, but he has given you an order to move, and by starting to move that is apparently what you are doing. The fact that the movement is not quite what he expected only confuses him more, thus giving you the slender advantage and the opportunity that is needed.

Pepper Spray and Liquid Gas Weapons

If the attacker produces an aerosol can and points it in your direction, this could be tear gas, oven cleaner, or just fly spray; it matters not, as they will all affect your eyes if you are hit in the face with the spray.

To reduce the possibility of damage to your eyes and give yourself a chance of escaping, follow these steps:

- Immediately turn away from the attacker and lower your head.
- Raise your shoulders in a shrugging motion.
- Hold your breath.
- Run as fast as you can away from the attacker's extended arm.

Whatever is in the can, whether it be tear gas or some other chemical, by turning away quickly you may prevent the stream from hitting you in the face, as this will be the area he is aiming for. Holding your breath as you run away will significantly reduce the possibility of inhaling the chemical whether it is deployed as a stream, fog, or mist.

The attacker runs the risk of gassing himself if he tries to follow, as he will have to run through the gas cloud to follow you. This is especially so if the irritant is discharged as a fog or mist.

There is always the possibility that some of the aerosol will affect you, especially if it is tear gas. If so, you will experience a burning sensation over any exposed skin, which may cause it to blister. In addition, you may have problems breathing, and your eyes will stream with tears and involuntarily shut with the intensity of the pain. If this happens, whatever you do, don't stop and attempt to wipe or rub your eyes. This will only spread the chemical and increase the level of irritation. The only way to gain some relief from this intense discomfort is to flush your face with cold water, and even this will give only a moderate level of relief. Cold milk has also been suggested, although this will probably be unavailable during a kidnap attempt.

Running with impaired vision, labored breathing, and an intense burning to exposed skin will be extremely difficult, but staying put will almost definitely guarantee a further dose of pepper spray and a successful abduction.

If you get hit with a burst of tear gas and you can't run away, immediately fall to the ground and completely relax your body. Falling down to the ground in a relaxed state serves two purposes. First, it is extremely difficult to lift someone from the ground when he or she is limp, and second, as the attacker attempts to grab you, he places himself within range for you to attack.

Once the attacker is close enough for you to attack, even from the ground, you are presented with numerous ways to fight back, including kicking his crotch, delivering an upward kick to the kneecap, or biting through the Achilles tendon. At this point, nothing should be out of bounds, and you should attempt anything that might disable your attacker.

If you have any sort of weapon at hand, this will be the right moment to use it. If it is a knife, stab him in the thigh, groin, or any area that you can reach. If you have a set of keys, rake the keys down his shin. If your weapon is a firearm, press it up against the attacker's body and fire. Accidentally hitting an innocent bystander if the bullet completely penetrates the attacker's body is always going to be a possibility. However, due to the close proximity of the attacker and the fact that you will be firing in an upward direction and at the same time pressing the weapon into his body, you will reduce this possibility quite considerably.

It should never be forgotten that you are fighting for your liberty and possibly even your life, so anything and everything goes, even biting. Although biting always comes with an attendant risk of AIDS, nowadays AIDS is treatable, and a dose of this may be far more preferable to being kidnapped, held for ransom, and then killed.

Stun Guns

Stun guns (see Figure 6.3) come in various forms (dealt with in greater detail in Chapter 9), but they are basically designed to discharge a low amperage/very high voltage (typically 50,000 volts) at a high pulse rate into the body. This rapid high-voltage discharge quickly immobilizes the body's nervous system, causing intense pain and loss of muscle control. However, as the amperage is very low, no permanent injury is generally inflicted. Those with heart problems or pacemakers have been known to have an adverse reaction to a stun gun discharge, but this rarely results in a fatality.

This low-amperage/very high-voltage energy delivered at a high pulse rate causes the muscles to work very rapidly but not very efficiently. The resulting energy loss results in a severe disruption to normal bodily functioning, disrupting the neurological impulses that direct muscle movement. This results in a complete loss of control over normal motor functions, leaving the recipient in a completely incapacitated condition for several minutes.

Figure 6.3   A high-voltage stun gun.

The following are general rules:

- A discharge of a quarter of a second will result in intense pain and muscle contraction.
- A one- to two-second discharge will increase the intensity of the pain and induce a disorientated mental state and severe muscle spasms, resulting in the recipient collapsing to the ground.
- A discharge over three seconds will just exacerbate the results of a one- to two-second burst.
- Anything over three seconds will result in severe disruption of the recipient's nervous system and total collapse. These effects will, even in very strong people, last for fifteen or more minutes.

As with tear gas, some people will be more affected than others. Those with weak hearts, pacemakers, or other medical conditions can suffer a heart attack, but this is seldom fatal.

Dealing with a Stun Gun Attack

To be on the receiving end of a stun gun attack is a very disturbing experience, and even an extremely strong and fit man will be completely disabled for as long as the voltage continues to be applied. You must also remember that the stun device need not be in contact with the skin to be effective, as the discharge will work even through thick clothing.

If the stun gun is one in which small darts on thin wires are fired at the victim, then the darts can be pulled out and discarded, but this may prove to be impossible. It must also be remembered that if the victim grabs

107

hold of the assailant, the victim will not be stunned, as the discharge is between the two darts and not the victim and the ground.

If you are shot with a stun gun, it will be all but impossible to do anything other than lie on the ground twitching until the stunning device is no longer discharging its current. Even then full muscle control will not return for some time.

If the stun device is one of the handheld type with two metal probes on the front, the discharge to the victim will be effective only as long as the probes are in contact with the victim. The only way of removing the contact with the probes is by lunging backward or twisting away. This will, however, be extremely difficult because of the lack of motor control that you will be left with. It may be possible to deliver a blow to the assailant that will cause him to drop the stun device, but this will be extremely difficult to effect. However, if you do manage this and the assailant drops the device, then you can pick it up and use it against him.

SOURCES

http://www.wikihow.com/Thwart-an-Abduction-Attempt.

http://naselfdefenseproducts.com/self_defense_information.

"Anti-Kidnapping Tips for Kids," video series, http://www.ehow.com/videos-on_5556_anti_kidnapping-tips-kids.html#ixzz26N3lo8wj.

http://www.articlesbase.com/self-defense-articles/techniques-to-help-survive-a-kidnapping-or-abduction-709725.html.

http://www.youthrights.org/community/forum/behavior-modification/regarding-self-defense-and-kidnapping.

W. E. Fairbairn, *Scientific Self-Defense* (Paladin Press, 2006).

John Townsend, *Self-Defense for Peaceable People: Defend Yourself Regardless of Size, Gender, Age, or Strength* (Blue Snake Books, 2006).

Rory Miller, *Facing Violence: Preparing for the Unexpected* (YMAA Publication Center, 2011).

ENDNOTE

1. brigacombatives.blogspot.com/.../universal-flinch-theory-picture-of.html; and "The Universal Flinch Theory: A Picture of Reality," www.policeone.com › Topics › SWAT.

7

Kidnapping from Ships, Oil Rigs, and Industrial Plants

KIDNAPPING FROM TANKERS, SHIPS, AND YACHTS

Piracy and kidnapping have existed for as long as the oceans have been sailed and utilized for commerce. They have affected people all over the world for centuries and have become a highly publicized threat impacting our communities, oceans, and coastlines that is not likely to wane soon.

Current Problem

Pirate activity and high-profile kidnappings off the coast of Somalia have added to the awareness of the problem for both large corporations and the long-distance sailing community in recent years.

Dealing with the problem presents a number of difficulties depending on the type of vessel targeted by these pirates. For sailboats and powerboats, simply avoiding those areas where piracy is a major problem will generally suffice. This advice is not, however, always adhered to, with predictable consequences.

For larger vessels, avoidance techniques may also include rerouting the ship's itinerary, but the attendant huge increase in fuel and crews' salaries often makes this financially nonviable. There is also the commercial aspect of the additional time involved with goods being delayed by weeks if not months. As such, lethal and nonlethal antipiracy countermeasures are often the only realistic ways to combat this threat to commercial carriers.

It must be remembered that the pirates are seeking anything of value, and for small vessels, that is, sailing ships and large motor yachts, that includes kidnapping the occupants of the ship for any ransom money that may be paid.

For larger ships, which include large tankers, bulk carriers, and cargo vessels, the Somali and other pirates are usually more interested in the value of a ship's cargo and what it might fetch for ransom than holding the crew for ransom. They are just not interested in protracted negotiations with the kidnap victims' government and their families. The cargo is worth millions of dollars, and so any kidnap victims are usually sold on to extremist groups such as Al-Qaeda, Al-Shabaab, or one of the other terrorist jihadist groups. This is where the real threat for the victim's life increases exponentially.

If a ransom is insufficient or involves protracted negotiations, then the victim will be executed. Even if the negotiations are satisfactory, the kidnap victim is still very likely to be killed, as the jihadist terrorists have little or no concern for any non-Muslims or any interest in the risky business of handing over the victim.

Under such circumstances, commercial carriers are forced into a situation where self-protection via lethal and nonlethal countermeasures is the only viable option to the financial penalties of rerouting their itinerary and the inherent risk to their crew.

NONLETHAL COUNTERMEASURES TO DETER PIRATES

Sound

Electronic equipment for the production of very high levels of sound can be used on small craft, which will include sailboats and powerboats.[1] With the larger power sources available on larger vessels, even higher levels of sound can be generated with such equipment. This high-pressure sound often exceeds 150 dB, which is louder than a jet engine.

The sounds produced by this equipment are so loud that they can cause nausea and permanent hearing loss and even burst the eyes. Such effects will almost always deter a pirate boat from its approach. One example is the American Technology Corporation's Long Range Acoustic Device (LRAD), which was developed to encourage pirates or protesters to disperse or, if they do not obey, to produce an extremely high-volume siren to drive them away.

Lasers

Eyes are far more vulnerable than ears, and high-powered lasers can be used to cause temporary blinding or even permanent damage to the eyes. Lasers are available in red, blue, yellow, violet, and green wavelengths, with green being the most damaging. The lasers used as pointing devices are normally in the red 1 mW power range, but some of the more recent handheld devices can be up to 1,000 mW. They can readily be purchased, even very high-powered ones, through the Internet at very reasonable rates.

Intelligent Optical Systems,[2] based in California, developed a strobe laser torch that makes targets dizzy and disoriented. Currently the effective range is only 15 meters, but development is ongoing. According to *The Economist*, "Laser Energetics, in New Jersey,[3] sells 'Dazer Lasers' that emit a green beam capable of dazzling people up to 2.4 km away."[4] And Wicked Lasers of the United States make a range of lasers in red, yellow, blue, and green, with power outputs of up to 750 mW.[5]

All of these high-powered lasers, especially those in the green spectrum, are valuable antipiracy tools and not particularly expensive.

Microwaves

The Active Denial System (ADS), which was developed by the U.S. military, works on the microwave oven principle, projecting a focused beam of electromagnetic radiation to heat the skin to 130°C.[6] This creates an intolerable burning sensation and attendant blistering that results in immediate incapacitation.

The U.S. military developed the Mob Excess Deterrent Using Silent Audio (MEDUSA).[7] As before, this uses a beam of microwaves, but this time it is pulsed, and the wavelength selected is designed to rapidly heat tissue, causing a shockwave effect inside the skull. MEDUSA's cranial audio effect is sufficient to cause extreme discomfort or even incapacitation.

High-Pressure Water and Additives

On larger vessels, high-pressure fire pumps can be used to cheaply and very effectively direct a high-pressure stream of water at approaching boats. Not only will this fill the vessel with water, but the pressure will be sufficient to knock the occupants out of the boat, deterring a piracy attempt. This can be an extremely effective and cheap antipiracy method.

111

To further enhance the effectiveness of the high-pressure hose, the water can be colored with a permanent skin dye. This has been found to be even more effective than water alone, as it immediately identifies those on the pirate boat. As the dye often takes weeks to wash off the skin, it can be a useful identifier once the pirates have reached land.

CN gas (see Chapter 9 for further details) when mixed in with the water from a high-pressure hose has been found to be extremely effective in riot control and would be equally effective in a pirate kidnap situation. The recipients of the water-CN water jet experience an extreme burning sensation under their armpits and in their groin area. The only slight relief from this pain is to stand with the legs wide apart and the arms raised. In this position it would be very difficult to continue with any act of piracy!

Another option to add to the high-pressure water is "Instant Marbles." This forms a film on anything it touches, rendering it so slippery that it is all but impossible to stand up on it. Once again, this would be highly effective when directed onto a small pirate boat.

Other Methodology

"Sticky foam" is an agent currently being used in Somalia by U.S. troops.[8] Sticky foam is used when less lethal force is required in a military situation and could be very effectively used in deterring a kidnap attempt by pirates. Sticky foam consists of extremely sticky materials carried in compressed form that are discharged with a propellant. It is an extremely effective, and nonlethal, method of entangling and deterring those involved in a piracy attack.

Another very cheap antiboarding measure is razor wire. Razor wire is indeed a very effective and cheap antiboarding barrier, but it is not easily removed for storage when entering port, and it corrodes in a sea salt environment.

The recently introduced "Guardian anti-pirate barriers" come in easily demountable units that will stack and can be stored on deck.[9] These are effective in the following ways:

- They provide a physical barrier around the guard rails of the ship or oil rig, which renders it almost impossible to climb over.
- It is also impossible to obtain a purchase for a boarding ladder of any type, as the barrier slopes away from the ship, causing the ladder to simply slip off.
- The barriers also prevent grappling hooks for obtaining a purchase, as they simply slide off.

LETHAL COUNTERMEASURES

These are the most commonly used counterpiracy and counterkidnap measures and include the use of firearms.

For small craft, firearms can serve as a deterrent and as a defense. On larger vessels, the use of firearms as piracy countermeasures may be limited by local and maritime law, as well as company policy.

Often the sight of a large gun proves to be a sufficient deterrent, without it ever having to be fired. In other cases, the very loud sound of a shotgun discharging serves as a deterrent. If shotguns are carried (see Figure 7.1), then they should be made of stainless steel, of the pump action type, 12 bore in caliber, and have a short barrel.

A pump action shotgun will be able to carry five or more rounds of ammunition in its magazine and have one round already loaded into the chamber ready to be fired. Pump action shotguns are of relatively simple design, and in the unlikely situation where a misfire or misfeed occurs, the pump action can quickly be operated to eject the defective round and load another into the chamber. After firing, a fresh round can be loaded into the chamber from the magazine by pulling back then pushing forward the fore-end. The spent round is ejected, a fresh round is loaded into the chamber, and the mechanism is recocked, ready for firing.

With most shotguns, the mechanism has a disconnecter that, after cycling the weapon's actions, prevents the weapon from being fired until the trigger is released and then pulled again. However, some pump action shotguns are designed to allow what is called "slam firing." Slam firing is when, if the trigger is held back rather than released after firing, the fresh round of ammunition fires as soon as the bolt closes onto the cartridge. Some Winchester shotguns, including the Model 870, are capable of firing in this way.

In normal situations, slam firing shotguns are considered to be unsafe, but when multiple rounds need to be fired very quickly, such as in a pirate attack, this mode of operation can be highly effective.

Figure 7.1 Stainless steel 12 bore pump action shotgun.

Ammunition Selection for Shotguns

A 12 bore shotgun can fire ammunition loaded with anything from a solid lead bullet of 0.729" (1.85 cm) diameter to dust shot. It can also be used to fire ammunition loaded with a bomb-shaped plastic missile loaded with tear gas, small lead-shot-filled beanbags, and rubber balls.

A very exotic type of ammunition that could have a severe psychological effect on anyone attempting to board a vessel is called "Dragons Breath." In this type of ammunition, the "missiles" consist of magnesium in dust, pellets, and shard form. When the round is fired, the magnesium ignites, causing flames to shoot out to over 100 ft. Resembling a flame thrower, it would have a severe psychological effect, especially at night (see Figure 7.2).

The author has found that for antipiracy and antikidnap situations, the magazine of the shotgun is best loaded first with a round containing number 9 size shot. This shot is the smallest generally available in 12 bore shotgun ammunition and is 0.08" (2.03 mm) in diameter. In a 2¾" length cartridge, there would be in excess of 600 of these very small lead pellets. Being so small and of relatively light weight, they would have little or no effect on a human being beyond twenty yards or meters. Firing one of these at a pirate boat would act as a warning shot not to come any closer.

If that has no effect, then the next round, or possibly two, should contain solid shot, that is, a single 12 bore sized (0.729" or 1.85 cm diameter) lead missile (see Figure 7.3). This would be effective against a human being up to ranges of 200 yards (182 m) or more and easily be able to penetrate the hull of a fiberglass or rubber-ribbed boat at this range.

Figure 7.2 A round of Dragons Breath ammunition fired at night.

Figure 7.3   Brenneke solid lead shot for 12 bore shotgun.

Figure 7.4   A flare gun.

The following rounds in the magazine should all contain SSG shot. A 12 bore shotgun cartridge loaded with SSG shot would contain eleven pellets each of 0.3" (0.76 cm) diameter. These would be effective up to 100 yards (91.44 m) and would be extremely effective against any pirates as they attempt to board the ship or have actually managed to climb on board.

It is often assumed that the spread of shot from a short-barreled shotgun is extremely wide. In fact, the spread is 0.729" (18.5 mm) at the muzzle and spreads out, with an unchoked barrel, a little more than 1" (2.54 cm) for every yard (0.9144 m) the shot travels. Thus, at 20 yards or meters, the shot spread would have a diameter of approximately 22 inches (54 cm).

If conventional firearms are not available, then a flare gun makes for an extremely effective antiboarding device (see Figure 7.4). Flare guns come in many forms, from the old WW2, 1" (2.45 cm) "Very Flare Guns" made entirely of steel to the modern commercially available weapons mostly made of high-impact plastic. A carefully aimed round into a pirate's boat would almost certainly set afire the boat or, even more dramatically, the fuel tank.

In extremis a flare round could be fired directly at those boarding, but this would have to be as a last resort, as the flare tends to stick to flesh and continue burning, with horrific results.

Illustrative Case

During the 1980s, Hong Kong was experiencing a dramatic rise in the use of very large high-speed boats to smuggle Mercedes Model SEL600 sedans from Hong Kong to China. These boats were generally powered by five 300 hp outboard engines and could reach speeds of more than 80 mph (130 kph), even with a large Mercedes 600 car on board.

Attempts to stop these boats all met with failure not only because of the speed they could attain but also because those on board were all armed with Chinese Type 56 (Kalashnikov AK47 variant) assault rifles. These were fired without compunction at the boats and helicopters attempting to stop them.

The boats, called Dai Feis (translation "Big Fast"), were all manufactured in small boatyards in Hong Kong specifically for the smuggling of these large and expensive cars. The boats were armor plated with thick stainless steel and bullet-resistant Makralon; however, the fuel tanks were often poorly made and leaked considerable quantities of fuel into the bilges.

During one chase, the special duties officer on board the helicopter fired a flare into the boat's hold. The flare set afire the fuel in the bilges, and there was a huge fireball that completely engulfed the boat. Eventually the flames set afire the 500 gallons of fuel in the tanks, with a dramatic effect. Both the boat and the car were destroyed and sank in deep waters without a trace.

OIL AND GAS RIGS

The threat level to workers on oil and gas rigs is small. There is little to attract terrorists, as the workers are generally not high-profile people of some wealth, as would be the case on cruise ships. And there is not much to be had in respect to holding the rigs themselves for ransom.

116

Standing on legs and being high out of the water, access is always going to be problematical. Antiboarding measures can, therefore, be fairly rudimentary, such as razor wire around the legs and safety rails. These rigs also have a plentiful supply of high-pressure hoses of more than sufficient power to deter the most determined boarder. If all else fails, there is always a plentiful supply of heavyweight workers!

Land-Based Gas and Oil Plants

The potential for armed attack and the kidnapping of workers and management is far greater at land-based plants than at similar production plants based at sea. They are often situated well off the beaten track, cover a vast area, and are vulnerable to attack by RPGs (rocket propelled grenades). The recent attack by jihadists at the Algerian Amenas gas installation is a prime example of the vulnerability of this type of installation.

The attack at the Amenas gas installation was well planned, with the sole intention of taking as many Western hostages, presumably for ransom, as possible. The attack took place as follows, according to the BBC:

- *Bus attack:* 05:00 local time 16 January 2013: A number of heavily armed militants attack two company buses that were carrying workers and staff toward the Amenas gas field. A Briton, an Algerian, and several locals die in the fighting.
- *Hostages taken:* The militants drive to the gas plant at Tigantourine and take Algerian and foreign workers hostage.
- *The Algerian army attacks:* 12:00 local time, 17 January: The Algerian army attack the militants as they attempt to move their captives from the Tigantourine facility in 4 × 4 vehicles. At that stage reports were sketchy but state that some hostages escape and others are killed.
- *Final assault:* The Algerians end the raid on 19 January, killing the last eleven kidnappers. During the attack, the kidnappers killed seven of the hostages. At least twenty-three hostages and thirty-two militants in total are known to have died.

Preventing such an attack would have been extremely difficult because of the size and remoteness of the plant and the fact that the workers were bussed in each day from villages outside the plant. To provide adequate armed guards for the bussing would have been possible, and this might have been enough to thwart the attack. However, without a substantial military presence to surround it, the plant would have been all but impossible to secure. Helicopter surveillance, a substantial twenty-four-hour heavily armed security force, and very good local intelligence will be the only way to prevent any such incidents in the future.

SOURCES

Intelligent Optical Systems, www.intopsys.com.

Laser Energetics, "Dazer Lasers," www.laserenergetics.com.

Steven H. Scott, "Sticky Foam as a Less-Than-Lethal Technology," *Proceedings of SPIE: Security Systems and Nonlethal Technologies for Law Enforcement* 2934 (January 29, 1997): 96–103 (John B. Alexander, Debra D. Spencer, Steve Schmit, and Basil J. Steele, Eds.).

Orion Flare Pistol, www.orionsignals.com.

www.brenneke-munition.de/cms/?L=1.

http://en.wikipedia.org/wiki/Shotgun_shell.

www.wickedlasers.com.

www.extremelasers.com.

ENDNOTES

1. www.marineinsight.com/.../18-anti-piracy-weapons-for-ships.
2. www.intopsys.com.
3. www.laserenergetics.com.
4. http://www.economist.com/node/21525838.
5. http://www.wickedlasers.com.
6. www.hqmc.marines.mil › News › News Article Display.
7. www.wired.com/dangerroom/2008/07/the-microwave-s/.
8. eandt.theiet.org/magazine/2011/08/one2ten-unusual-weapons.cfm.
9. marineautosecuritysolutions.com/latest_news.htm; "Algeria Crisis: Hostage Death Toll 'Could Rise,'" BBC, http://www.bbc.com/news/world-africa-21106795.

8

Personal Protection
Body Armor

BULLET-RESISTANT VESTS

Body armor might not be the first thing that comes to your mind when considering antikidnap protection. Kidnappers are, after all, out to capture you and demand a ransom from your family, loved ones, or government; they have no interest in anything else other than the money. You are, therefore, worth more to them alive than dead, and shooting you is definitely not on their agenda. However, any attempt at avoiding kidnap and/or trying to escape could result in the kidnapper opening fire to wound you and stop you from escaping. A bullet-resistant vest (BRV) is, therefore, a sensible and probably essential item of personal protection when in a kidnap hotspot.

HISTORY

Body armor, in the form of metal plates covering most of the body, was widely used in medieval times during the time of hand-to-hand combat with swords and lances. With the advent of the crossbow and more especially the firearm, plain steel suits were found to be incapable of defeating the steel bolts and lead balls, and they rapidly became obsolete.

During World War II, *ballistic nylon* (a copolymer of the basic polyamide) was used against shrapnel from grenades and small bombs. This was, however, of little or no use against even slow plain lead bullets.

119

The major advance in soft body armor came with a generation of what are loosely referred to as *super fibers*, which were introduced by DuPont. The best known of these was a para-aramid fiber called Kevlar,[1] which was originally used in fabric-braced radial tires. However, it did not take long for it to be realized that these extremely strong fibers could be woven into a fabric that was so strong that it could be used in bullet-resistant soft body armor.

The Kevlar fibers were simply woven into sheets, with varying thicknesses of yarn and density of weave (called *denier*), to provide the particular properties required. The sheets were then assembled into ballistics panels that were further reinforced with Kevlar cross-stitching. The panels thus formed were permanently sewn into a carrier in the form of a vest.

It is undeniable that Kevlar does produce a very effective, lightweight, and flexible vest that can be tailored to stop virtually any handgun missile. It does, however, suffer from a number of problems. First, it is not stable to UV light and has to be kept inside a lightproof pouch. Second, it is very susceptible to attack by acid and many household chemicals, and third, if wet it loses most of its ability to stop bullets.

A recent development in the field of soft body armor is the use of an ultra-high molecular weight polyethylene fiber called Spectra,[2] which is produced by Allied Signal Inc., and Dyneema,[3] which is produced by DSM Inc. These are basically the same and consist of exceedingly fine-spun fibers of ultra-high molecular weight polyethylene. These fibers are laid in dense mats at 90° to each other then covered top and bottom with a thin sheet of polyethylene. This is then heat treated to semimelt the fibers together or bonded with a plastic resin to form a sheet. With the thousands of bonded fibers that must be pulled from the matrix to allow the passage of a bullet, these sheets are even more efficient than Kevlar. This material is not affected by water (in fact it floats), it is not affected by UV light or any chemical, and it is considerably lighter than Kevlar. If it has a disadvantage, it is that its melting point is somewhat lower than that of Kevlar.

One of the most recent innovations in bullet-resistant materials concerns the use of materials that exist as a semisolid under normal circumstances, but when they are subjected to a shock, such as a bullet strike or knife attack, they solidify. These are called *shear thickening materials* (or dilatant materials) and are composed of hard particles suspended in a liquid. The liquid is generally polyethylene glycol, and the particles are nano-sized pieces of silica. This shear thickening liquid is soaked into the layers of a normal Kevlar vest and can reduce the weight of the vest by up to a third. As Spectra and Dyneema cannot be wetted, they cannot be used with sheer thickening liquids.

Lawrence Bonk of Crunchwear.com reported that BAE Systems in Bristol, United Kingdom, conducted tests in which metal projectiles were fired at over 300 m/sec into both thirty-one layers of untreated Kevlar and ten layers of Kevlar combined with the liquid. These tests determined that the liquid-treated armor was as effective as the much thicker untreated one.[4]

MECHANISM OF BULLET-RESISTANT MATERIALS

To effectively stop a bullet, the material must first deform the missile. If the surface area of the bullet is large enough and the material has sufficient resistance to the passage of the bullet, then the energy transfer to surrounding fibers can occur, and the bullet will stop. A nondeformed bullet will merely push apart the weave and penetrate.[5]

If the bullet is sufficiently soft, that is, plain lead, semijacketed, or thinly jacketed, then the material alone will often be sufficient to cause the deformation. If, however, the bullet is heavily jacketed or of the metal-penetrating type, then some intermediate, much more rigid material will be required to deform the bullet. This generally takes the form of a hard plate that fits in front of the soft body armor. These are called *ballistic inserts*.

Ballistic Inserts

This is the name generally given to rigid plates that are placed in front of the soft body armor. Their purpose is to break up high-velocity, hard-jacketed, and metal-penetrating missiles. Once the bullet's velocity has been reduced and its shape deformed, the underlying Kevlar or Spectra material will easily stop it. These inserts are generally made from either a fused ceramic material, heat-treated aluminum, hardened steel, or titanium alloy. These can be either solid plates or small overlapping tiles.

More modern materials such as hot-pressed boron carbide and silicon carbide are also being introduced, which considerably reduce the weight of the insert. One problem with such ceramic and boron carbide plates is that they shatter when struck by a bullet, thus losing much of their stopping potential for a second round. Soft body armor is not infallible, as the following two cases illustrate.

Illustrative Case

The first case involves a police officer wearing a very substantial BRV capable of defeating .357" Magnum and 9 mm PB caliber bullets. He was shot at close range with a .45-70 rifle that had a large soft bullet weighing 400 grains at a velocity of 1,500 ft/sec (457 m/s). Although the jacket was successful at defeating the bullet, the bullet and BRV were driven into the officer's chest, killing him instantly.

Illustrative Case

The second case involves a live demonstration of a ballistic insert plate made of steel. The plate was designed to defeat an armor-piercing round, but the demonstration was merely to show how effective it was against a full magazine from a submachine gun. The soldier wearing the jacket was not killed, but the fragments generated by the bullet breaking up on the plate completely severed the lower part of his jaw.

STANDARDS FOR BRV THREAT LEVELS

Body armor standards are regional, as the ammunition used in criminal activities varies from country to country, and the standards are set to reflect this. As a result, the armor testing must reflect not just the local threat but also, to a certain extent, the climatic conditions. For example, in tropical climates where there is heavy rainfall, the local specifications might include waterproofing the jacket of the pouch in which the ballistic panels are contained.

Research shows that in a large number of cases where law enforcement officers are shot and injured or shot and killed, the officer's own gun is the offending weapon. As such, many law enforcement or paramilitary agencies will set their own requirements for armor performance and protection based on their own firepower—ensuring that the armor will at least protect against their own weapons' firepower.

There are many standards for body armor. For example, the Home Office Scientific Development Branch (HOSDB) in the United Kingdom and the National Institute of Justice (NIJ) in the United States provide standards and protocols. These are often used by many countries as baseline standards. However, other countries sometimes modify these standards to satisfy local crime concerns, the weaponry used, and the climatic conditions.

The British Home Office standards for bullet- and stab-resistant vests are listed in Appendix 3, and the NIJ standards for BRVs are listed in Appendix 4. The NIJ standards for stab-resistant body armor are listed in Appendix 5.

CONSIDERATIONS TO BE TAKEN
WHEN CHOOSING A BRV

The first and most important is, obviously, are you going to be shot at? Kidnappers are out to capture you and demand a ransom from your family, loved ones, or government. The kidnappers will have no interest in anything else other than the money they might obtain from your capture. You are, therefore, worth more to them alive than dead, and they are very unlikely to shoot you. That is not to say, however, that once the ransom has been paid, they will not kill you anyway! Handing you over to family, friends, or the police involves great risks for the kidnappers. During debriefing you can describe kidnappers' ethnicity, possibly their religion, any names you might have overheard, what sort of property you were being held in, some indication of the property's location, how many kidnappers were involved, whether others were being held captive, and so on. If you were particularly astute during your captivity, you might even have managed to obtain a sample of the captors' DNA from saliva or blood. If you have been captured by terrorists, the chance of your being killed is far greater than if the kidnappers are a local criminal gang. The simple fact is that you must do everything in your power to avoid capture in the first place, and if that involves the possibility of being shot at by a thwarted kidnapper, then a BRV is an essential piece of equipment.

The second consideration is determining what level of BRV is required. It is no use having a 30-lb BRV with built-in metal plates capable of defeating an armor-piercing rifle round if all the local kidnappers are using .38″ Special caliber revolvers. Local knowledge of the criminals and terrorists, the weapons they are likely to use, and their modus operandi is, therefore, essential.

The third consideration is the mobility and wearability of the chosen BRV. Even a lightweight BRV is going to restrict your movement, to say nothing of being extremely uncomfortable in 30°C temperatures. This problem can be alleviated to some extent by wearing specialized underwear, some of which have a built-in cooling system. Even something as simple as a traditional string vest can substantially decrease this problem. Some manufacturers can produce a suit or overcoat in a BRV material. While this might be less cumbersome than a standard BRV worn under a suit, it will not be able to provide the same level of protection. This reduced level of protection results from the restricted number of layers of Kevlar or other material that can be fitted into a BRV suit or overcoat and still have it look as it is supposed to.

The fourth consideration is whether the BRV going to be worn inside a suit (covert, as shown in Figure 8.1) or outside (overt, as shown in Figure 8.2). BRVs designed for wearing over clothing can be much more substantial and easily be fitted with steel plates, pockets for radios, and so on. They do, however, make it extremely obvious that you are wearing one. The thinner, covert type of BRV is much less conspicuous, as it can be worn under a shirt. It is undeniably lighter and easier to wear, but it will be far less capable of stopping bullets than an overt BRV.

Last, consider whether a stab-resistant vest (SRV) may be sufficient. SRVs are, apart from being very much thinner, visually indistinguishable from a covert BRV. The SRV is generally worn under other items of clothing and is designed to resist knife attacks to the chest, back, and sides. They are also extremely efficient in protecting against blunt trauma, for instance, in a car crash.

Normally, an SRV would not be considered as being sufficient to ward off a kidnapping attempt by a criminal using a firearm, as most SRVs afford little protection against high-powered bullets or those with a hard jacket, although they may defeat a low-velocity plain lead bullet such as a

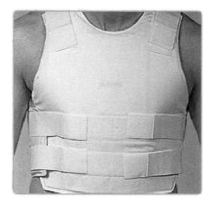

Figure 8.1   Covert bullet-resistant vest.

124

Figure 8.2 Overt bullet-resistant vest.

.38" Smith & Wesson caliber round. SRVs are designed to prevent serious injury by stopping a knifepoint from penetrating more than a few milli-meters. SRVs are also syringe, needle, and slash proof. Note that terrorists, and even relatively unsophisticated criminal gangs, will not generally use a knife in a kidnap attempt, as a bladed weapon could easily result in the victim being accidentally mortally wounded, which is something the kid-nappers definitely don't want.

These SRVs come with various minimum performance ratings. In the United Kingdom, the rating is defined under the HOSDB publication No. 39/07/C. In the United States, the NIJ has established a stab-resistant body armor test standard (NIJ Standard 0115.00). See Appendixes 3 and 5.

In addition to this, a BRV will possess a considerable defense against a bladed weapon. The author has, on numerous occasions, attempted to penetrate the lightest weight of BRV (NIJ Level 1) with ice picks and razor-sharp hunting knives. Never once has the blade or pick penetrated more than a few layers of the Kevlar or Spectra.

A lightweight SRV may be ideal for beat police officers or wardens in a jail and can be considerably cheaper than a BRV, but it is never going to be a match for a BRV in a kidnap situation.

SOURCES

K. G. Sellier and B. P. Kneubuehl, *Wound Ballistics and the Scientific Background* (Elsevier, 1994).

R. A. Poole, R. E. Cooper, L. G. Emanuel, L. A. Fletcher, and I. C. Stone, "Angle: Effect on Hollow Point Bullets Fired into Gelatin," *AFTE Journal* 26, no. 3 (1994): 193–98.

"New Shear Thickening Fluid (STF) Enables Flexible, Comfortable Armor," http://www.gizmag.com/go/5995/.

John Croft and Daniel Longhurst, *HOSDB Body Armour Standards for UK Police (2007): Part 3: Knife and Spike Resistance,* Publication No. 39-07-C (Home Office Scientific Development Branch, 2007).

Joe McGonegal, "What's the Future of Armor: Liquid or Solid?" *Slice of MIT,* August 7, 2013; http://alum.mit.edu/pages/sliceofmit/2013/08/07/whats-the-future-of-armor-liquid-or-solid.

"Ballistic resistance of body armor," *NIJ Standards* (U.S. Department of Justice, July 2008).

B. L. Lee, T. F. Walsh, S. T. Won, H. M. Patts, J. W. Song, and A. H. Mayer, "Penetration Failure Mechanisms of Armor-Grade Fiber Composites under Impact," *Journal of Composite Materials* 35, no. 18 (2001): 1605–33.

E. K. J. Chadwick, A. C. Nicol, J. V. Lane, and T. G. F. Gray, "Biomechanics of Knife Stab Attacks," *Forensic Science International* 105, no. 1 (1999): 35–44.

"Taking the Stab Out of Stabbings," *TechBeat* (Spring 2000), 1.

The Home Office Departmental Report 2005 (June 20, 2005), 19.

J. Smith and I. Greaves, "The Use of Chemical Incapacitant Sprays: A Review," *Journal of Trauma* 52, no. 3 (2002): 595–600. PMID: 11901348

Uwe Heinrich, *Possible Lethal Effects of CS Tear Gas on Branch Davidians during the FBI Raid on the Mount Carmel Compound Near Waco, Texas, April 19, 1993* (The Office of Special Counsel John C. Danforth, 2000).

H. Hu, J. Fine, P. Epstein, K. Kelsey, P. Reynolds, and B. Walker, "Tear Gas: Harassing Agent or Toxic Chemical Weapon?" *JAMA* 262, no. 5 (1989): 660–63.

wikipedia.org/wiki/Tear_gas.

www.nij.gov/topics/technology/body-armor.

ENDNOTES

1. www.dupont.co.uk/products-and-services/fabrics-fibers.../kevlar.html.
2. www.spectra-group.co.uk.
3. www.dyneema.com/.
4. Lawrence Bonk, "BAE Systems' Shear-Thickening Liquid Makes for Lighter Armor," July 8, 2010, http://www.crunchwear.com/bae-systems-shear-thickening-liquid-makes-for-lighter-armor/.
5. www.wiley.com › Home › Life Sciences › Forensic Science. Brian J. Heard, *Handbook of Firearms and Ballistics: Examining and Interpreting Forensic Evidence,* 2nd ed. (Wiley Blackwell, 2008).

9

Personal Protection
Weapons

Everyone equates weapons with guns and knives, and while they are viable self-protection options, in many jurisdictions the carrying of such weapons without a permit is illegal. There are, however, legal alternatives, once again depending on the jurisdiction, that can be carried without your having to apply for a license.

Carrying a metal nail file is perfectly acceptable in all jurisdictions that I know of, and this can be used against a potential abductor with great effect as a weapon for stabbing or raking across an abductor's face or eyes. A good sturdy ballpoint pen can be very effectively used to seriously damage the eyes or even, if used with sufficient force, in a stabbing action to penetrate the chest wall. There are also small-edged weapons called "push daggers" that are manufactured by several companies, including Cold Steel.[1] These can be attached to a key ring and used very effectively against an abductor. Any knife larger than this will be too bulky to carry, will take time to deploy, and could breach local laws on the carrying of edged weapons.

PERSONAL (RAPE) ALARM

Bringing an abduction attempt to the attention of as many bystanders as possible is always going to be far better than shooting or stabbing an abductor. A personal alarm, often referred to as a rape alarm, is a cheap and effective way of obtaining the notice of those around you.[2]

127

These small alarms emit a high-pitched and very loud noise, often in excess of 140 dB, that can be heard up to a half a mile away. Many such rape alarms are also fitted with a bright Xenon strobe light that, at night, can temporarily blind an attacker. The main advantage of rape alarms is that they are not, as far as the author is aware, restricted in any country.

TELESCOPIC STEEL BATON

Telescopic steel batons come in various sizes, all of which will telescope down to a compact size and can be kept either in a belt pouch or preferably in an inside pocket specially designed for holding this type of weapon (see Figure 9.1).[3]

These batons can be quickly deployed with a flick of the wrist and, with a little training, can be a very effective weapon for self-defense. They can be used in a stabbing motion but are far more effective when used in a slashing action.

Figure 9.1   A telescopic baton.

To effectively use such a weapon, you will need to be about a foot (30 cm) farther away from where you can just strike the opponent. This will allow you to step forward and strike with the added momentum of your forward momentum but be out of the range of the attacker. If necessary, you will be able to take a farther step back and use the baton in self-defense.

The best target areas for a baton are the neck, groin, and areas where the bones are closest to the surface of the body, that is, wrists, hands, elbows, collarbone, and knees. A hard strike from a steel telescoping baton can easily break a wrist.

The legal situation regarding the carrying of batons varies greatly by country, and steps should be taken to ensure that the local legislation allows the carrying of such concealed weapons. In the United States, the carrying of a steel baton or other type of club varies from state to state. For example, Vermont and Arizona allow the legal carrying of a baton for self-defense, whereas others such as California have restrictions against the carrying of all club-type weapons by non-law enforcement personnel. These states will, however, often make exceptions for security guards.

According to the U.K.'s Prevention of Crime Act 1953, instruments that are created or adapted for the purpose of causing personal injury are considered offensive weapons. Batons and telescopic batons, which fit this profile, have been banned as a result of the Criminal Justice Act 1988, which prohibits their manufacture, sale, and import.

Canadian law also has a similar ban. Section 90 of the Criminal Code makes it illegal to carry any kind of baton if carried in a concealed manner. Spring-loaded batons are considered a prohibited weapon and so are banned altogether. Private citizens in Sweden are allowed to own any kind of baton but cannot carry the baton in public in accordance with their legislation 1988:254. The legislation may be different in kidnap hotspots in other parts of the world, and exemptions and some latitude may be shown to persons at high risk.

If difficulties are experienced in legally carrying a baton, spring loaded or otherwise, then a heavy, well-constructed flashlight, such as a Maglite, can be as an effective weapon as a baton.

TEAR GAS

Tear gas, defined as a lachrymatory and/or sternutatory agent (i.e., creates tears and causes breathing difficulties, coughing, and sneezing), is a nonlethal chemical agent that causes severe irritation to the eyes, causing tears, extreme pain, and even blindness. Blistering of the skin is also a common result in those with fair or sensitive skin. In extreme cases, especially if the person is an asthmatic or suffers from breathing difficulties, large doses can lead to death.

Common lachrymators include pepper spray (oleo capsicum [OC], an extract of chilies), CS gas (2-chlorobenzalmalononitrile), CN gas (phenacyl chloride), bromoacetone, syn-propanethial-S-oxide (from onions), and Mace (a branded mixture).[4] Of these the only ones that are likely to be generally encountered in a commercially available spray are CS gas, OC, and Mace. The rest are more appropriate to military or security force use.

Commercial sprays are available in CS and OC forms, but undoubtedly the most useful, as far as personal protection is concerned, is OC. This is because while CS is a far more effective spray against human beings, it has absolutely no effect on dogs. In those countries where rabies is rife, carrying an OC spray is highly desirable for that use alone.

The tear gas in aerosol spray cans is generally in liquid form to be discharged as a jet, a spray, or a powder. It can also be loaded into cartridges as a powder for use in revolvers and self-loading pistols specifically designed for firing blank and tear gas ammunition.

TEAR GAS SPRAYS

These sprays come in many types and sizes, from very large fire-extinguisher-sized containers for use in riot situations and by prison guards to very small units that will fit on a key ring. The key ring units contain only a small amount of the chemical and give a limited number, usually about twenty-five, discharges of gas.

Tear gas canisters are available to discharge the gas as an aerosol or as a stream. Of the two, the stream is the more effective, as it can be aimed directly into the eyes rather than just sprayed as an aerosol cloud, much of which will miss the target.

Larger sizes of spray often contain a gelling agent to ensure that the tear gas sticks to the attacker. As the tear gas exits the container as a gel, it also has a greater effective range that can be twenty feet or more. Pepper spray should always be directed toward the assailant's face at as close a range as possible and should never be sprayed wildly, especially in a crowded area.

The pain of having OC or CS sprayed into the eyes is intense, and most recipients fall immediately to the ground. The eyes will involuntarily shut and be all but impossible to open until the effect has worn off. Most people react to being sprayed by tear gas by rubbing their eyes, which only makes the effect worse, as it simply pushes the liquid further into the skin. The only relief obtainable, other than by waiting for an hour or two until the effect wears off naturally, is by washing with cold water or even milk.

If you are forced into a situation where a tear gas spray has to be utilized, you must be very careful to avoid becoming your own victim by way of the gas cloud being blown back toward you by the wind. Try also to avoid contact with the assailant once he has been sprayed, as the chemical on his clothes or skin can easily transfer to you, causing extreme discomfort or incapacitation.

If you do become contaminated with pepper spray, rinse the affected skin or the eyes repeatedly with cold water. As the residue can be quite oily, baby shampoo can sometimes be effective in removing it from the face and hair. Baby shampoo, even if the product is advertised as being tearless, should not be used to remove the tear gas from the eyes. Any contaminated clothing will require washing several times, but care should be taken not to wash with uncontaminated clothing.

Many countries ban the carrying of tear gas sprays, and local legislation should be consulted to ascertain the legality or otherwise of their use.

TEAR GAS GUNS

These guns can be of either the revolver or the self-loading pistol type and are generally of .22", .25", or 8 mm caliber. Revolvers of .38" caliber have also been manufactured, but because of their bulk, they have found little favor. All weapons designed for firing tear gas ammunition have a forward-pointing barrel with some form of obstruction to prevent missiles from being fired.

Guns specifically designed for firing blank cartridges, that is, for starting races, usually have a false, blocked barrel with an upward-pointing vent angled at about 45° away from the firer. Although tear gas ammunition can be fired from blank-firing weapons, there is an inherent risk of the firer receiving as much tear gas as the intended victim.

Tear gas ammunitions always have a red colored wax plug in the case mouth to distinguish them from blank-firing cartridges, which usually have a clear colored wax plug. Cartridges for use in nail driving guns are very similar in appearance to tear gas ammunition and have a colored card in the case mouth to indicate the strength of the cartridge. This can be red in color, but it is always a card and never wax. Tear gas cartridges, as mentioned previously, are generally of small caliber and contain only a relatively small quantity of tear gas. Their effective range is, therefore, quite limited.

Tear gas guns, like tear gas sprays, are also restricted in many countries. In the United Kingdom, for example, they are classified as "prohibited weapons" and are restricted to the same extent as submachine guns.

STUN GUNS

Stun guns come in various forms, but they are designed to discharge a low amperage/very high voltage (typically 50,000 volts) into the body. This discharge quickly immobilizes the body's motor functions, causing intense pain in the process. However, as the amperage is very low, no serious or permanent injury is generally inflicted.

This low amperage/very high-voltage discharge causes the neurological stimuli that direct muscle movement to be short-circuited. This results in a loss of muscle control, disorientation, and a loss of balance. The recipient will almost certainly fall to the ground and be unable to regain control for up to fifteen minutes. Even then he may remain in a dazed and disorientated state.

While the actual effect will vary from person to person, the following are general rules:

- A discharge of a quarter of a second will repel and startle the recipient and cause considerable pain and muscle contraction.
- A one- to two-second discharge will cause intense pain, muscle spasms, and a dazed mental state, often causing the person to drop to the ground.[5]
- A discharge over three seconds will cause pain that is even more intense and in addition will cause loss of muscle control and disorientation.
- Any discharge over three seconds will cause the person to fall to the ground and be unable to recover for fifteen minutes or more.

As with tear gas, some people are more affected than others, and those with weak hearts or other neurological conditions can suffer a fatal heart attack.

Types of Stun Guns

Two main types of stun guns are currently available:

- One type of stun gun fires two darts attached to the weapon via very thin electric cables. These cables conduct the charge to the victim.
- The other type includes handheld devices that have two prongs that are pushed against the victim to deliver the charge.

Of these types of guns, the weapons that fire darts are generally used only by the police and security personnel. They are only loaded with, at the most, two sets of darts and are not at all suitable for personal protection, as they are large and cumbersome.

The type of weapon where the charge is delivered via the exposed prongs comes in many forms from something resembling a flashlight, to cigarette packet sizes, to large hand-sized weapons.

More recent developments in the field of stun weapons include one that, instead of using thin wires to carry the electricity, uses a thin stream of salt water. There is also an experimental type fired from a 12 bore shotgun. This is essentially a self-contained version of the stun weapon with the two prongs, but it is fitted into a 12 bore projectile. This has a much greater range than the Taser-type weapon and can be used up to 100 feet.

Illustrative Case

A 12 bore stun projectile was used in the Raoul Moat siege case in 2013 in the United Kingdom.

Raoul Moat was a body builder whose excessive use of steroids built up huge muscles, at the expense of his mental stability. After being released from an extended stay in prison, he proceeded to shoot three people with a sawed-off shotgun, one of whom was a police officer. After six days on the run, he was cornered in a field but refused to give himself up. He was shot twice with 12 bore stun rounds, but they proved ineffectual. Eventually, he committed suicide by shooting himself with the 12 bore sawed-off shotgun.

FIREARMS

Undoubtedly, a firearm is the most effective weapon to ward off a kidnapper. Merely pulling one out of a holster will almost always be sufficient to ward off a potential kidnap situation. One must, however, be proficient in the use of firearms, and in particular the one being carried, and be completely prepared to use it if the occasion arises.

When selecting a firearm for personal use, you have, realistically, only two candidates to consider:

- A self-loading pistol
- A revolver

Before you select the most suitable candidate, you need to learn about these two types of weapons.

Self-Loading Pistol

In this type of weapon (see Figure 9.2), the ammunition is contained in a removable spring-loaded magazine usually housed within the grip frame. The barrel of the weapon is surrounded by a slide with an integral breechblock that is kept in the battery (i.e., when the face of the breechblock is up tight against the breech [rear] end of the barrel in a position ready for firing) by a strong spring.

Pulling back the slide allows the topmost round of ammunition in the magazine to present itself to the rear of the barrel. When you allow the slide to move forward under spring pressure, the round is pushed, by the bottom of the breechblock, from the magazine into the chamber of the barrel. This action also cocks the trigger mechanism. When you pull the trigger, the hammer drops and the round is fired, pushing the

Figure 9.2   Colt .45″ caliber self-loading pistol.

bullet down the barrel. The slide is forced to the rear by the equal opposite force on the base of the cartridge case by the gases that drive the bullet down the barrel. As described in the National Research Council's book *Ballistic Imaging*, as the slide moves to the rear, "the spent cartridge case is ejected through a port in the side, or occasionally top, of the slide. At the end of its rearward motion," the spring-loaded slide moves forward again, "stripping a fresh round off the top of the magazine and feeding" it into the chamber at the rear of the barrel, ready for firing. As the action is only self-loading, the pressure on the trigger has to be removed and then reapplied before another round can be fired.

To prevent the weapon from firing continuously, a part of the action, called a *disconnecter*, removes the trigger from contact with the rest of the mechanism. Releasing the trigger disengages the disconnecter, allowing the trigger to re-engage with the mechanism so that a fresh round can be fired.

This type of weapon is available in many different calibers, from the very small .22" and .25" calibers up to very large and powerful .44" Magnum calibers.

Revolver

In a revolver, each round of ammunition is contained in its own chamber in a cylinder at the end of the barrel. Cocking the hammer rotates the cylinder via a ratchet mechanism to bring a new round of ammunition in line with the barrel. Pulling the trigger drops the firing pin onto the cartridge, thus firing the round. This is the simplest type of revolving pistol mechanism and is called the "single action" mode of operation. The earliest types of revolving pistol employed this type of mechanism. A good example of a single action revolver is the Colt Single Action Model of 1873 (see Figure 9.3).

Figure 9.3 Single Action Army revolver.

Figure 9.4   Colt Police Positive Double Action revolver.

The other type of revolving pistol mechanism is called "double action." In this design, a long, continuous, and relatively heavy "pull on the trigger cocks the hammer, rotates the cylinder, then drops the hammer all in one operation."[6] Most modern revolvers employ this type of mechanism, with virtually all of them having the capability for a single action mode of operation as well. An example of a double action revolver is the Colt Police Positive revolver (see Figure 9.4).

WEAPON TYPE SELECTION

When you are selecting a firearm for self-protection, the main consideration is ease of use. There is no point in having a huge weapon firing a Magnum round of ammunition that is capable of taking out a human being at 200 yards when any encounter is likely to be within a few yards. Likewise, a weapon designed for target use with all the attendant muzzle weights and extra heavy barrel will be of no additional use at close range. The weapon of choice must be small, easy to use, and capable of firing a round not of huge power but sufficient to incapacitate a potential assailant.

Although a .22″ caliber weapon is capable of killing a human being, it will not have the shocking power that one requires to incapacitate a person. A .38″ Special caliber revolver or a .380″ K (9 mm Short) self-loading pistol is sufficient for such close range personal protection.

Self-Loading Pistols

Self-loading pistols are very flat, have a large magazine capacity, and are available in many calibers. They do have one major drawback in that they are quite complicated to use. They can be carried loaded with a single round and ready to go, but there is, despite modern safety mechanisms being extremely reliable, always the chance of a mishap. Weapons with an external hammer are best carried uncocked and with a round of ammunition in the chamber. "Hammerless" weapons can be carried loaded, cocked, and ready to fire, as the hammer is enclosed and less likely to be jarred off than a weapon with an external hammer.

If the weapon were carried uncocked and unloaded, the slide must be pulled fully to the rear and then released. This chambers a round from the magazine and cocks the mechanism ready to fire. In times of stress, this can often lead to a misfeed, which jams the gun, or even a nonfeed, where nothing is fed into the chamber. Self-loading pistols are also quite complex pieces of machinery, and unless they are kept meticulously clean, they can easily malfunction.

A self-loading pistol is not, in the author's opinion, an ideal weapon for self-defense. Should, however, it be deemed that a self-loading pistol is preferable, the caliber should be carefully selected. A .22" or .32 ACP (7.65 mm) round, as featured in the early James Bond 007 films, has far too little stopping potential for use as a self-defense weapon. Realistically, a .380" (9 mm Short) cartridge would be far better, but even this is marginal. Anything larger than this and the weapon becomes far too bulky to carry as an undercover weapon. It should be noted here that hollow point, fully jacketed bullets do not expand at all well at the speeds achieved by self-loading pistol cartridges of this caliber.

Revolvers

A revolver is a superior choice for use in a close range kidnap situation. The reasons for this include the following:

- Revolvers are far less complicated than self-loading pistols.
- With the mechanism predominantly inside the frame and with few exposed moving parts, a revolver is far less likely to malfunction from the ingress of dirt and debris.
- Revolvers can be carried with all chambers loaded and the hammer in the uncocked condition, ready to fire in double action mode.
- Revolvers do not, generally, have a safety mechanism that must be deactivated before the weapon can be fired.
- Revolvers all have highly reliable built-in safety mechanisms that are disconnected as soon as the trigger is pulled.

- As a result of the inherent strength of the revolver's frame, much more powerful rounds can be fired than from an equivalent-sized self-loading pistol.
- With a double action revolver, the trigger simply requires a long, relatively heavy pull to rotate the cylinder and cock then drop the hammer onto a round of ammunition, thus firing it. If in the unlikely situation of a round not firing, all that needs to be done is to pull the trigger again and a fresh round will be presented to the firing pin for firing.
- There is no possibility of a jam through misfeeding a round from the magazine.
- If the situation presents itself where it is necessary to take a more precise aim and the situation allows time to do this, then the hammer can be manually cocked for a single action mode of firing. Single action firing allows a much shorter and lighter pull on the trigger, resulting in increased accuracy.

SELECTION OF CALIBER AND WEAPON

This is a very personal matter, but because the author has carried a weapon for many years, he can make a few generalities.

- The weapon must be concealable and not too heavy. Carrying a large bulky weapon in a shoulder or belt holster soon becomes tiresome, to say nothing of being very uncomfortable.
- Aluminum-framed weapons should be avoided, as this limits the power of the cartridges that can safely be fired.
- The barrel should be short to aid in deploying the weapon and to reduce its weight. There is no need for a six inch barrel with its inherently more accurate attributes over a short barrel. All confrontations will be at a short range, probably no more than six feet. A barrel length of two or three inches would be ideal.
- It must be capable of firing cartridges of sufficient power to ensure that the assailant is disabled. A .22" caliber revolver is light and small, and the ammunition is more than sufficient to take out small game. It is, however, unreliable for larger targets such as a human being. The caliber should, ideally, be of .38" Special caliber and of the "+P" type. The .38 Special+P ammunition is about 30 percent more powerful than standard .38" Special

Figure 9.5 The grooves in a hollow tipped bullet allow the point segments to "splay out" upon impact, inflicting more damage than a nonhollow point.

caliber ammunition but can still safely be fired in steel-framed .38" Special revolvers.

- The bullets should be of the hollow point (often wrongly referred to as Dum-Dum bullets) type (see Figure 9.5). Hollow bullets are designed to expand on impact with soft targets thus increasing the wounding effect of the bullet. The velocity of a standard .38" hollow point bullet is too low to reliably expand; however, .38" Special+P bullets are much faster, and the hollow point bullets will generally expand. This expansion results in a far greater wounding effect and thus shocking ability than a non-expanding bullet.
- The weapon should be as resistant to corrosion as possible. A weapon carried under the armpit in a shoulder holster or even in an inside or outside belt holster is subject to considerable humidity, to say nothing of the additional corrosive effects of sweat. In a tropical climate with temperatures of 35°C and 95 percent humidity, a normal steel "blued" weapon will begin to corrode very rapidly. Attempting to prevent this by applying large quantities of oil will make the weapon slippery to handle, probably render the ammunition inoperative, and cause bad rashes on the skin of the wearer. The ideal type of weapon would, therefore, be one made entirely of stainless steel.

Of the weapons available there are many, but the author's preference is a Smith & Wesson Model 60 stainless steel five-shot revolver with a two-inch barrel (Figure 9.6).

The last consideration is the holster. There are many options to choose from as to where the gun is to be carried: inside belt, outside belt, shoulder, ankle, or even crotch. Of these, the simplest type of holster is always going to be the most preferable, and on the basis of the author's experience, an outside belt holster is ideal (see Figure 9.7).

Figure 9.6   Smith & Wesson .38" Special Caliber Model 60 revolver.

Figure 9.7   Outside belt holster.

A weapon will serve its purpose only if it is ready to be used instantly. If a person has chosen to carry a weapon but keeps it in his or her purse, backpack, or even pocket, by the time it is out and ready for use, it will probably be far too late.

SOURCES

Major Julian Hatcher, *Textbook of Pistols and Revolvers* (National Rifle Association, 1935).

War Office, *Textbook for Small Arms 1929* (Naval and Military Press, 2009).

Handgun Wounding Factors and Effectiveness (U.S. Department of Justice, Federal Bureau of Investigation, 1989).

Martin L. Fackler, Book Review, "*Street Stoppers: The Latest Handgun Stopping Power Street Results,*" *Wound Ballistics Review* 3, no. 1 (1997): 26–31.

Shawn Dodson, "Reality of the Street? A Practical Analysis of Offender Gunshot Wound Reaction for Law Enforcement," *Tactical Briefs* 4, no. 2 (2001).

Jerry Lee, *Gun Digest 2014* (Gun Digest Books, 2013).

Gun Digest Illustrated Guide to Modern Firearms (Gun Digest Books, 2012).

Massad Ayoob, *Gun Digest Book of Concealed Carry* (Gun Digest Books, 2012).

ENDNOTES

1. www.coldsteel-uk.com.
2. www.personalalarms.com.
3. www.weapons-universe.com/Personal.../Expandable_Batons.shtml.
4. www.mace.com/mace-pepper-spray.../mace-triple-action-personal.html.
5. http://jonbenetramsey.pbworks.com/w/page/11682467/Evidence%20 of%20a%20Stun%20Gun.
6. National Research Council, *Ballistic Imaging* (National Academies Press, 2008); http://www.nap.edu/openbook.php?record_id=12162&page=30.

10

Weapons Likely to Be Used by Kidnappers and Terrorists

Kidnappers hardly ever fire guns, as the whole concept of a kidnap is to end up with a live hostage. If a firearm is used, then it will be as a weapon of intimidation. This will be against either the intended victim or anyone who might attempt to intervene. For intimidation purposes, the kidnapper's weapon will normally be much larger than a weapon used primarily as a self-defense weapon.

The choice of weapon depends on many factors, including in which country the kidnap takes place, whether a relatively unsophisticated criminal gang or a professional terrorist group does it, and what the perceived target value is.

In Western countries, for example, Canada, approximately only 19 percent of kidnap cases involve the use of firearms, whereas in Eastern European and South Asian kidnap hotspots, for example, Afghanistan, where terrorists compose the majority of the kidnappers, the proportion approaches 100 percent.

As to the weapon of choice, if it is a small-time gang or individual, then the weapon of choice would generally be a cheap .38″ caliber revolver. More professional kidnappers would be armed with a self-loading pistol, together with tear gas or a stun gun of some type. If a terrorist group is carrying out the kidnapping, then the weapon choice has no bounds and is almost certainly going to involve an AK47 (Kalashnikov) of some description.

Kidnapping and piracy is altogether a different game, as the perpetrators, whether Somali or other groups in the Indian Ocean, can obtain their weapons of choice from any of the unstable countries in the region. Many come from Yemen, a hotbed of terrorist activity. A significant number of weapons will also have come from Mogadishu, the Somali capital, by a very complex route. This will involve weapons dealers in Mogadishu who receive a deposit from a *hawala* dealer (Islamic money broker) which has originated from the pirates. The weapons are then driven to Puntland (a region in northeastern Somalia) by a third party. It is here that the pirates pay the balance and finally take possession of the weapons.

Various photographs of pirates indicate that their weapons are predominantly AKMs, RPG-7s (rocket propelled grenades), AK47s, Chinese Type 56s, and semiautomatic pistols such as the Russian TT33 or Chinese Type 54. They are also likely to have hand grenades such as the Soviet RGD-5 rifle grenade or F1 hand grenade. The use of an RPG or rifle discharged grenade against an oil tanker would have serious consequences.

The rest of this chapter provides a short list of weapons that have been utilized by terrorists.

SMALL ARMS

Most of the small arms used by pirates and terrorists are of military origin, but hunting weapons are also occasionally encountered.

- Common calibers of pistols
  7.65 mm
  7.62 mm
  9 mm PB (parabellum)
  .45″ ACP
- Common calibers of assault rifles
  7.62 × 39 mm
  5.45 × 39 mm
  7.62 × 54 mm
  .223″ (5.56 × 45 mm)

Manufacturers

The list of weapons that have been used by terrorists and kidnappers includes virtually every manufacturer known, as well as virtually every type of weapon that is or has been made. The most common weapons used include the following.

The TT33 Soviet self-loading pistol in 7.62 × 25 mm caliber: It was designed by Fedor Tokarev in 1930 but was not adopted into Soviet service until 1933 (see Figure 10.1). It is basically a Browning design but with some modifications to economize the manufacture. The 7.62 × 25 mm cartridge has a relatively small bullet (7.62 mm diameter bullet and 25 mm long cartridge case) that has a heavy steel jacketed bullet. This bullet construction results in a missile that can easily penetrate a bullet-resistant vest designed to defeat .357″ Magnum ammunition.

A Russian M20 pistol was also manufactured that was exactly the same as the TT33 except that it had no markings on the weapon at all and was intended for clandestine sales. It was also manufactured under license by China (Type 51 and 54), Poland (wz33), Hungary (M48), and Egypt (Tokagypt).

AK47 Soviet assault rifle: The AK47 in caliber 7.62 × 39 mm was adopted by the Soviet Army in 1949 as its standard issue assault rifle. It was superseded by the AKM in 1959 (see Figure 10.2). During the cold war, the USSR supplied countless arms, mainly AK47s, to anti-Western insurgent terrorists, and as such the AK47 became a symbol of left-wing revolution.

Figure 10.1   Chinese Type 54 pistol (same as Soviet TT33 self-loading pistol).

Figure 10.2   AK47 Soviet 7.62 × 39 mm assault rifle.

It is estimated that "between 30 and 50 million copies and variations of the AK47 have been produced world wide,"[1] making it the most widely used rifle in the world. What makes this weapon so popular is that it is almost indestructible, and if badly damaged it can often be repaired by the local blacksmith.

Probably the most common variations of the AK47 is the AKM.[2] This is an updated version of the AK47 designed for modern manufacturing techniques. It was introduced into service with the Soviet Army in 1959 and is available with both a solid stock (AKM) and a folding stock (AKMS). The version most often seen is the folding stock version (see Figure 10.3) because of its short length and ease of use.

It has been stated that if you give a terrorist a sophisticated modern weapon (e.g., the American M16), he will turn it into a useless piece of junk in a very short time. Give him an AK47 and it will become the most effective weapon in the world!

RPG-7: The Russian RPG-7 is the most widely used antiarmor weapon in the world because of its simplicity, low cost, and effectiveness against soft- and hard-skinned vehicles (see Figure 10.4). It has been issued to the forces of the former USSR, the Chinese military, North Korea, and any country that received weapons and training from the Warsaw Pact.

The RPG-7 is used extensively by almost all terrorist organizations and is on the inventory of many insurgent groups and is available at very low cost through illegal international arms markets, particularly in Eastern Europe and the Middle East.

Figure 10.3 AKMS folding stock version of the AKM assault rifle.

Figure 10.4 RPG-7 (rocket propelled grenade).

OTHER WEAPONS LIKELY TO BE UTILIZED IN A KIDNAP SITUATION

Knives

A knife will always be a good weapon for a kidnapper because of the traumatic psychological effect it will have on the victim. A kidnapper will generally be very wary of actually using a knife because of the distinct possibility of inflicting a mortal wound to his victim. This is something the kidnapper will want to avoid at all costs, as a dead kidnap victim will possess absolutely no money-generating potential at all.

The more aggressive looking the knife is, the more of a psychological effect it will have on the victim. A small kitchen knife or folding penknife will be of little use in this respect.

Tear Gas Sprays and Stun Guns

These are also widely utilized by both terrorists and local gangs to subdue their victims. These are dealt with in greater detail in Chapter 9.

SOURCES

Douglas Farah and Stephen Braun, *Merchant of Death: Money, Guns, Planes, and the Man Who Makes War Possible* (Wiley, 2008).

Andrew Feinstein, *The Shadow World: Inside the Global Arms Trade* (Jonathan Ball Publishers SA, 2013).

Charlie Cutsha, *The New World of Russian Small Arms and Ammo* (Paladin Press, 1998).

Jerry Lee, *Gun Digest 2013* (Gun Digest Books, 2012).

Will Fowler, Anthony North, Charles Stronge, and Patrick Sweeney, *The Illustrated World Encyclopedia of Guns* (Lorenz Books, 2010).

Frank C. Barnes, *Cartridges of the World*, ed. Richard Mann (Gun Digest Books, 2012).

Leland S. Ness and Anthony G. Williams, *IHS Jane's Weapons: Ammunition 2013–2014* (Janes Information Group, 2013).

Terry J. Gander and Ian Hogg, *Jane's Guns Recognition Guide* (Collins Reference, 2005).

ENDNOTES

1. http://www.ak-47.net/ak-47/ak47.php.
2. James F. Gebhardt, *The Official Soviet AKM Manual* (Paladin Press, 1998).

11

Survival on Being Kidnapped

The chances of your being kidnapped are small, and even if it does happen, your chances of survival are high. Kidnapping is unquestionably a petrifying experience, but with some mental fortitude, it is possible to cope with the situation far better than you might realize.

Although it may be of little comfort when you are under the extreme duress of being held as a hostage, you must never forget that you are of value to your abductors only if you are alive. That they will want to keep it that way is beyond doubt. Experience has likewise shown that the longer you are held in captivity, no matter how onerous it may be, the better the chances are that you will be released alive.

Being mentally prepared will enable you to overcome the shock of being kidnapped despite it likely being the most distressing experience that you have ever had to endure. A 9-to-5 busy but comfortable and secure life will suddenly be changed into a terrifying situation of forced inactivity and isolation. It is inescapable that you will have to endure degradation and extreme discomfort for however long it takes for you to be freed.

The transition from your safe and secure existence to captivity will have been violent in the extreme, and you will probably have suffered some sort of serious but non-life-threatening injury. There is also the distinct possibility of your driver or some of those around you having been killed.

You will be stripped of your clothes, given rags to wear, and forced to use a bucket or hole in the ground to perform your bodily functions. To add to the indignity of it all, your captors will probably take great delight in watching while you perform. To add to the mental trauma, you will never know, especially if terrorists are holding you, whether you will be tortured or killed.

The only way of coming out from the other end of this ordeal with any degree of sanity is to have previously thought and planned for such an outcome and to have placed this planning into effect during your time in captivity. You should have discussed, in advance, the possibility of kidnap with your spouse, the security personnel at your place of work, and possibly the consulate.

The more you know about kidnapping, the less fear you will have of the unknown. Research has shown that only about 3 percent of kidnap victims are killed.[1] Unfortunately, most of those who were killed were done so during the actual abduction, poorly executed escape attempts, or an inept rescue attempt. While some hostages are held for a long time (some have been held for years before being released on payment of a ransom), the vast majority of kidnaps are successfully brought to conclusion in fewer than five days.

From the instant of capture, you should do everything you can to remain calm and alert. Only by doing so will you be able to make those mental notes regarding your captors and surroundings that are likely to help the police at a later date. Do not provoke your kidnappers or, even worse, laugh at them, as this will only make your life that much more miserable and almost certainly lead to a beating.

You should do your utmost to fix in your mind their faces, voices, dress, and characteristics and the number of persons and their gender who were involved in the kidnap. Particulars of any vehicles that were involved, such as their make, model, and color, will provide additional information that will be required by the police.

If you are psychologically prepared for the abduction, you will be better able to discipline yourself and concentrate on committing this information to memory rather than on agonizing over why it happened.

As Richard Clutterbuck wrote in his seminal treatise *Kidnap and Ransom: The Response*, the victim

> will probably be forced face down on to the floor of the car so that he cannot see, and he may later be transferred into a closed van, or have his eyes covered and his ears plugged. Nevertheless, he should fix in his mind any clues he can get about his route: time, speed, distance, sharp turns, gradients, traffic lights etc.; and any sights or sound he is able to detect, such as crossing a railway or passing close to the airport; also the direction of the sun. If he has an idea whether he went north

or south, he may possibly find a way of communicating this during negotiations, or in written or taped messages he is ordered to send out; even if he cannot do that, the information may help in arresting the gang later.

He should also try to detect the kind of place into which he is taken: e.g. into a garage with inside access to a suburban house, the car park under a block of flats, the back entrance of a shop, or a workshop or a warehouse. If the gang is a professional one, the likeliest eventual hide-out (probably after at least one transfer between vehicles, and perhaps also after a brief spell in a transit lockup) will be a house, flat or garage in a quiet, prosperous suburb, which may offer more choices of getaway route than an isolated farmhouse. Again, the victim should consciously store sights, sounds and smells in his memory. At least one hostage contributed to the eventual capture of his kidnappers because he could hear aircraft taking off from a small and recognizable airfield; and another by remembering details of the wallpaper.

The treatment of the victim in the first few days after capture is likely to be at its most brutal, calculated to humiliate and demoralize. He may be injected with some drug such as scopolamine, designed to relax resistance and loosen the tongue. Geoffrey Jackson [a U.K. diplomat kidnapped in Montevideo, Uruguay, in 1971] countered this drug by disciplining himself to talk fluently to the point of verbosity on unimportant issues and, if cornered on important ones, to attempt to blur his answers with more verbosity, in such a way as to make the two indistinguishable.

Your interrogators are likely to use "good cop–bad cop" techniques, contrasting brutality and kindness, light and dark, noise and silence. They will probably make attempts to mentally disorientate you with sensory deprivation by keeping you in the dark and permanently blindfolded with your ears plugged. As you will have no means of telling the time of day or whether it is day or night, be eating unpleasant food at irregular times, and be lacking sleep, your mental state could very quickly deteriorate. You must overcome this initial period of brutality by coming to the realization that this is probably going to be the worst part of your captivity and reminding yourself that the great majority of hostages do survive this period.

During interrogation you must be particularly careful not to reveal anything about the likely reactions to your capture by your family, company, or government. During this initial interrogation, you will almost inevitably be asked for the telephone number of someone to ring and tell him or her about your kidnapping and the kidnapper's demands for your release. This will require much thought on your part, as the initial reaction by the recipient to the kidnappers' call can influence all subsequent negotiations.

You should also avoid discussion about how much money your family has and how any ransom money might be raised. Any such information will help the kidnappers assess the level at which to make their first demand. You should avoid any attempt at negotiating the size of the ransom that the kidnappers are demanding. They might just consider that a small sum will be insufficient to be worth keeping you alive. The probable outcome will be to kill you there and then.

OBSERVE YOUR CAPTORS

Right from the start, be observant. Remember every single detail that you can; this will not only assist in your escape, should you so try, but also supply information to the police that will aid in apprehending and convicting the kidnappers. Although you may be blindfolded, you still have your senses of hearing, touch, and smell, which can all assist in gathering important information.

Useful observations include the following:

- How many kidnappers are there?
- Are they armed? If so, with what?
- Are they in good physical shape?
- What do they look and/or sound like?
- Can you ascertain their country of origin from their accent?
- How old are they?
- Are they well prepared not just for the kidnapping itself but also for your subsequent incarceration?
- What is their emotional state?

OBSERVE YOUR SURROUNDINGS

- Where are you being taken: a house, barn, garage, commercial building?
- Try to visualize the route taken by the abductors to assist in recalling the details at a later stage.
- Make note of the number and direction of turns, stops, and variations in speed.

- Try to estimate the time between points of reference, that is, a railway crossing and a set of traffic lights.
- Try counting between each turn, for example, 128 left, 12 right. Counting out a second as "1,000" will assist in this estimation.

What Sort of Premises Are You Being Held In?

Gather as much information as you can about your surroundings that may be helpful if you decide to escape.

- Is it a lockup, bungalow, farmhouse, building, derelict warehouse?
- If it is a house, how many rooms are there?
- How old is the building?
- What floor of the building are you being held on?
- Are the floors to each level concrete or wood?
- Is there an elevator, and from its sound where is it in relation to where you are being held?
- Where are the exits, and how many are there?
- Are there fixed closed-circuit television cameras in place?
- What type of lock is on the door?
- Does the door have a padlock?
- Are there any other security precautions?
- What obstacles are there, such as a large settee or table and chairs, that might obstruct those sent to rescue you?
- Try to figure out what part of the city you are being held captive in.
- Try to distinguish between smells, as this may give an indication as to where you are being held (i.e., in a town market, farm, industrial estate).
- Listen to the sounds of activity in the building.
- Listen for sounds out in the street.
- Is there a mosque or church nearby?
- In what direction is the mosque or church?
- Is there a street market nearby?
- Are there any clues or smells that may give you an idea as to the type of market (i.e., livestock)?
- Is the location on a bus route, and is there a bus stop nearby?
- Is the property in a quiet residential area or a down-market and noisy street?
- Is there a flyover nearby?
- Is there an airport nearby?

- What types of aircraft are flying from the airport: heavy passenger planes, light aircraft, helicopters, military planes?
- Is it possible to estimate the distance to the airport?
- In what direction are the planes taking off?

OBSERVE YOURSELF

- Are you injured or wounded?
- With what are you restrained?
- How much freedom of movement do the restraints give you?

Try to ascertain from those holding you why you have been kidnapped. Motivations for kidnap are many (i.e., sexual assault, ransom demands, political leverage). The motivation for your kidnap could determine whether you attempt to escape and, if caught, what the likely outcome will be. If your kidnappers are common criminals, then the retribution meted out will not be as severe as if they are terrorists. With terrorists, it could, if you are caught, be terminal for you.

If you are being held for ransom, you are worth far more to them alive than dead, as nobody is going to pay for the release of a dead body. But, as has been previously stated, if terrorists are holding you, there is a substantial risk of your being killed after any ransom has been paid.

Expect to be accused of being an undercover agent seeking intelligence on the kidnappers and to be brutally interrogated. Do not volunteer information or make unnecessary proposals, and definitely never admit to being an undercover agent.

If a sexual predator has abducted you, your abductor will, after obtaining whatever gratification he seeks, almost certainly kill you. In such a situation, escape is a priority. Likewise, if you've been abducted for some political or military action or the release of political prisoners, then it is probable that you will, eventually, be killed. Your decision to attempt an escape must be made with this in mind. If you are likely to be killed at some stage, then an escape attempt should be made as soon as practically possible.

What to Do If You Are Interrogated

- Retain a sense of dignity, but cooperate as much as possible.
- Divulge only that information that will not incriminate you in their eyes.

- Do not say anything that is likely to embarrass your government, as this could be very counterproductive as far as your rescue is concerned.
- Do not be inflexible or antagonize your captors, as this will most likely result in your getting a beating.
- Concentrate on surviving.

KNOW YOUR CAPTORS

- Memorize their schedule.
- Look for patterns of behavior that may assist in your escape.
- Identify the strongest character among your captors, and look for weaknesses or vulnerabilities within the group. This may assist in your search for escape opportunities.
- Establish a connection with your captors. Family, sports, and hobbies are universal subjects.

Your aim is to convince your kidnappers that you are not just a sum of money awaiting payment but a person with whom they can identify. Empathize with the kidnappers' concerns, but never discuss or praise their cause. Try, if you can, to converse in their language, as this will give you some common ground and generate a bond. Learning the language will also assist you in understanding what is happening with regard to your situation and any negotiations regarding your release.

Do not complain about your food or the conditions under which you are being kept. Do not, no matter what the provocation, become argumentative or quarrelsome, and attempt to obey all instructions no matter how offensive they may become.

Once you have established some degree of understanding with your kidnappers and they start to view you as a person rather than simply as a captive, you can ask for some latitude regarding the conditions of your incarceration. You could ask for the odd item that will improve your situation, such as additional food, books, papers, or a blanket. Any medicines you require should be brought to their attention as soon as practically possible. These requests should be made not in an overly antagonistic way but in a reasonable and nonconfrontational manner and with the reminder that you could fall seriously ill and die if they are not available. They will not want this to happen.

From the onset you should anticipate that your stay will be lengthy, and it is essential that you keep some track of time. If you are in a windowless room, then changes in temperature and mealtimes will give an indication of day and night. These should be recorded in the established way of drawing on the wall six vertical and one horizontal line equating to one week.

A daily routine is essential, which must include periods of mental and physical exercise. Even if you are in cramped situations, isometric exercises, squats, and push-ups will assist in keeping your muscles in good shape. Should the occasion arise for an escape, you will need to be in as fit a condition as possible, so these exercises are essential. To retain your fitness, you must eat whatever you are given, no matter how repulsive it may seem.

You will achieve some measure of mental well-being by contacting other hostages who might be present in the building. Your guards will probably react with violence should they discover any such contact, so it is imperative that your attempts at communication are not discovered.

INTERROGATION

You should strive to be cooperative during your interrogation, and you should not become hostile toward your interrogators no matter how tempting this may be. Any such behavior will almost certainly result in your being held for longer than would normally be expected and result in beatings and probably torture.

Be helpful and civil, and preserve your self-control. Whatever you do, do not lose your temper, and make your responses short and to the point. Most important of all is not to offer up information. Talk about the weather, football, tennis, or any other noncontroversial matter. Do not become involved in discussions about religion or politics, and do not fall for the "good cop–bad cop" technique that they will inevitably attempt.

Be aware of the "Stockholm syndrome." This occurs when the captive begins to empathize with his or her captors and their cause and can progress to the point where the captive actively embraces and becomes part of their fight. The Patty Hearst kidnapping case is the prime example of the Stockholm syndrome.

SURVIVAL ON BEING KIDNAPPED

Illustrative Case

The Patty Hearst kidnapping case in 1974 is the prototypical example of the Stockholm syndrome. Patty Hearst gained notoriety when she joined the radical left-wing group, the Symbionese Liberation Army (SLA), after having been kidnapped by them.[2] She can be seen in Figure 11.1 in this well-known photograph of her holding a weapon, robbing the Hibernia Bank in San Francisco on April 15, 1974.

You could well be forced to present your captors' demands to the police or your country's embassy. This could be in writing but more probably via a video recording. You will be given a script to read out for the recording. Avoid ad-libbing your own request for help. Any attempt to alter their prewritten message will almost certainly result in your receiving a severe beating.

Be patient, and remember that hostage negotiations are often difficult and time-consuming. Many previous kidnaps have proved that your chances of survival will increase the longer you are held captive and that the majority of kidnappings end without loss of life or injury.

Figure 11.1   An armed Patty Hearst at the Hibernia Bank, San Francisco, April 15, 1974. (*Source*: FBI.)

RESCUE AND ESCAPE

It is most probable that you will eventually be released or rescued unharmed. If you do make an escape attempt, do not do so unless you are certain of success. If you try and are successful, go directly to your nearest consulate and seek protection. If you cannot reach your own consulate, then a consulate belonging to a country friendly to your own is the next best option. If this is impossible, then the local police will have to be trusted.

As any rescue attempt will be made only after negotiations have failed, the lives of everyone involved in the rescue will be at risk. If a rescue attempt is made, it will probably be by Special Forces. Once they have entered the room where you are being held, the first thing they will do is shout for everyone to drop to the floor. You must do this immediately, as the rationale is that the kidnappers or terrorists will be trained to fight, and they will continue standing. This will immediately identify them, and they will almost certainly be shot! You must, therefore, keep a low profile and immediately follow all instructions. The terrorists may well attempt to disguise themselves as hostages, but ignoring the shouting for everyone to lie on the floor should identify them. If you do not follow their instructions to the letter, then your getting shot is a real possibility.

Precautions to Take During a Rescue Attempt

- Do not attempt to run away.
- Drop to the floor, lie face down with your hands crossed over your head, and remain still. If for some reason that is not possible, put your hands on your head, drop to your knees, and remain still.
- Do not make any sudden move that a rescuer may interpret as being hostile.
- Obey all instructions that you are given, and do them instantly.
- The rescuers may initially regard you as a terrorist or kidnapper, but just stay calm until the initial confusion is over.
- You may well be handcuffed and searched, but do not under any circumstances resist, as you may be shot.

POST-KIDNAPPING TRAUMATIC SHOCK SYNDROME

As Clutterbuck wrote, "Post-kidnapping shock is a major physiological and psychological problem"[3] that will need addressing upon your release. No matter how strongly you feel that it is not required, it is a process that needs seeing through. Being unprepared for the mental trauma associated with post-kidnapping shock will only make the situation markedly worse. It is, therefore, of paramount importance that while you are in captivity, you keep your morale as high as possible. The kidnappers will do their utmost to bring about complete dominance over you. You must continuously resist this by retaining your dignity and a sense of self-esteem.

SOURCES

Geoffrey Jackson, *Surviving the Long Night: An Autobiographical Account of a Political Kidnapping* (Vanguard Press, 1974).

David Boulton, *The Making of Tania Hearst* (New English Library, 1975).

Vin McLellan and Paul Avery, *The Voices of Guns: The Definitive and Dramatic Story of the Twenty-Two-Month Career of the Symbionese Liberation Army, One of the Most Bizarre Chapters in the History of the American Left* (Putnam, 1977).

"Surviving Kidnapping," http://danger.mongabay.com/kidnapping.htm.

Judith Tebbutt, *A Long Walk Home: One Woman's Story of Kidnap, Hostage, Loss—and Survival* (Faber and Faber Non-Fiction, 2013).

Paul Chandler, Rachel Chandler, and Sarah Edworthy, *Hostage: A Year at Gunpoint with Somali Gangsters* (Mainstream Publishing, 2011).

Chris McNab, *Hostage Rescue with the SAS (Elite Forces Survival Guides)* (Mason Crest Publishers, 2002).

ENDNOTES

1. Richard L. Clutterbuck, *Kidnap and Ransom: The Response* (Faber and Faber, 1978).
2. www.crimelibrary.com/terrorists_spies/terrorists/hearst/1.html.
3. Clutterbuck, *Kidnap and Ransom*. See also http://www.medicinenet.com/script/main/art.asp?articlekey=12516 and "Hostage Survival," https://mcalvanyintelligenceadvisor.com/hostage-survival.

12

Post-kidnapping Debriefing

Few life experiences are as difficult and challenging as being kidnapped. However, knowledge of the stratagems for coping with being kidnapped can increase your chances of survival and enhance your health and safety during captivity and release. It will also assist in the dissemination of vital information pertaining to the kidnappers and their modus operandi, which could be vital in assisting the investigation of future kidnaps, to say nothing of bringing those involved to trial.

While there is great variability in the behavior of kidnappers toward their victims, there are a number of basic areas that should be expected. An appreciation of these areas will assist you in surviving the period of incarceration and the subsequent post-traumatic stress period and assist with the debriefing and dissemination sessions.

These basic areas are as follows:

- Physical restraint and sensory deprivation (i.e., being handcuffed and blindfolded)
- Mental cruelty
- Violent interrogation
- Brainwashing to induce a Stockholm-type situation
- Verbal abuse and humiliation
- Threats of death and mock executions
- Physical abuse or, in the case of sexual perverts, sexual abuse and rape

A review of the literature reveals that there are six stages of adaptation to captivity,[1] all of which have a profound effect on the victim's behavior after release. These stages are as follows:

1. Confusion and severe anxiety as a result of the kidnap
2. Disbelief that he or she could have been kidnapped
3. Increased perception and apprehension
4. Defiance and/or acquiescence with the kidnappers' demands
5. Dejection or depression
6. Recognition and acceptance of the situation

The period of time over which these stages occur lengthens progressively from the first stage to the final stage. More specifically, the first stage lasts only seconds to minutes, and the second stage lasts minutes to hours. The third stage generally lasts a few hours to a few days, and the fourth stage lasts from several days to a few weeks. The fifth stage is more protracted, lasting several weeks to a few months. Finally, the sixth stage can last anything from several months to many years.

A general description of each stage follows, together with reference to kidnapper and victim behavior and mention of some coping practices.

STAGE 1: DISORIENTATION

This is the first stage, which lasts from seconds to minutes. This stage is influenced greatly by the setting in which a captive is taken. Kidnappings are almost always unexpected and can be life threatening. It is the abrupt transition from normality to sudden, often brutal, subjugation that is difficult if not impossible for the victim to comprehend. Typical reactions include a fight-or-flight response, uncontrollable trembling, and confused and nonrational thinking.

Such a transition is impossible to quickly assimilate, even for those who have gone through kidnap training. In addition, the victim has fear for his or her life and the lives of others during these first seconds to minutes.

At this stage, the kidnappers are generally highly excitable and driven by ideological and/or religious causes, and the victim may well be at a loss of how to cope. Any challenge to the kidnappers' actions at this juncture, even by a laugh or sneer, can lead to brutal retaliation and even execution.

162

It is the extreme brevity of this stage that makes it extremely difficult for the victim to cope with this stage of the kidnapping. The victim must try to regain his or her coordination and control of the concomitant anxiety as quickly as possible. Some victims manage to cope with the initial shock via a dissociated state, feeling more like observers than participants in the kidnap. Others can be in a state of stunned shock, unable even to move let alone take any positive action. If victims have an ability to focus their minds on the details of the situation, they can greatly assist in limiting these negative responses to the stress of being kidnapped.

STAGE 2: DISBELIEF

The second stage will last from minutes to hours. Victims who are used to protection via Western law with an emphasis on human rights may well respond with utter disbelief when they are suddenly thrust into a situation where all personal freedoms and rights are forcibly withdrawn. The initial mental response to this is invariably, "This is only temporary, and I'll be rescued very soon." Deep down in his or her subconscious, the captive will understand that it is not temporary, and rescue will be a long time coming.

At this juncture, the kidnappers' behavior can be abysmal toward the victim and can include the use of restraints and severe beatings. In addition, the captive will have his or her clothes and all personal possessions taken and be blindfolded. While the victim is in this degraded and disheveled condition, it is probable that a photograph will be taken for future propaganda or ransom use.

At this stage, the kidnappers' plans for the victim are frequently unstable, with the group moving the victim from one location to another. This can occur any number of times, not just to disorientate the victim but also to throw any would-be rescuers off the scent. Victims often cope with this stage by convincing themselves that conditions will shortly improve. During this stage, the victim's hope for rescue may help his or her mental state, but it is often a forlorn hope. Inwardly the victim will be fuming with outrage at the situation into which he or she has been placed, and thoughts of retaliation are common. This is, however, counterproductive, and thoughts should be more tranquil, possibly about family and friends. Victims have reported that even if they are not religious in nature, prayer has helped them cope during this period of their incarceration.

STAGE 3: HYPERAWARENESS AND ANXIETY

The third stage lasts from hours to days and refers to the situation whereby the captive is extremely wary and alert to minute details. Being easily startled by any unusual noise or sudden movement is another symptom, and it is a common tendency to think the worst of any situation that may arise.

During this hypervigilant stage, victims may discover unexpected powers of observation probably brought on by the extreme stress under which they find themselves. Remembering convoluted and complex routes through city streets and having an ability to accurately keep track of passing time are just two of the many skills that frequently present themselves.

The kidnappers' behavior during the first few days is likely to be unpredictable, as they may well be confused over their ultimate objectives. At this stage, they will probably begin some form of intense interrogation to gather intelligence as to whom they should contact regarding a ransom demand and how much they should demand.

Logically it may seem prudent to attempt an escape during this initial and confused period. Any such attempt should, however, be put on hold during these early days of captivity, as the guards will be in a heightened state of alertness, especially regarding any such possible escape attempt.

During this hyperalert period, captives can turn these powers toward orientating themselves to the place they are being held and, if blindfolded or in a dark room, constructing a twenty-four-hour cycle to keep a tally of their incarceration period. It is very easy at this stage for captives to misinterpret small snatches of overheard conversation by their captors. This could lead to unnecessary disappointment and despair when, for example, they misinterpret the kidnappers' words as being indicative of their early release or rescue.

STAGE 4: RESISTANCE AND/OR COMPLIANCE

This fourth stage usually lasts from a few days to several weeks. During this stage, the captive's behavior varies greatly from individual to individual. Some are totally incapable of dealing with even minor pressure from their captors, whereas others are easily able to resist even the most intimidating and/or bullying tactics.

During this stage, captors will usually demand that the captive sign a confession of some description or make a video to promote their cause. It is best not to fight against these demands, and under no circumstances should captives attempt to ad-lib with their own message. Any attempt to do this will result in a severe beating.

During this period, the captors will utilize isolation to wear down their victim into compliance. The conditions will almost always be cramped, filthy, and ridden with vermin and fleas. The temperature will be extremes of hot and humid and cold, with poor or no lighting and ventilation. There will also be little in the way of privacy or personal hygiene. "Good cop–bad cop" interrogations will be interspersed with long periods of isolation, with the interrogations happening at any time of the day or night.

The sole aim of this treatment is to break captives' will and make them compliant to the demands of their captors. Some victims will attempt to resist all attempts at intimidation until they are thoroughly beaten and broken, even to the point of death. Others prove to be incapable of enduring even moderate degrees of poor treatment. However, most captives do eventually learn to overcome torture, isolation, and other deprivations until severe physical and/or psychological damages become a serious threat to their well-being. Before it reaches this critical stage, most captives do comply with their captors, which results in a suspension of the deprivations, allowing victims time to rest and recover. One tactic that can often provide a brief respite from the torture and beatings is to provide information that will take a long time to validate.

One of the easiest and most productive coping techniques is to increase one's physical fitness. Even in very confined accommodations, it is possible to carry out quite extreme bouts of physical exercise. Isometric exercises to increase flexibility will reduce the risk of joint dislocations and bone fractures during bouts of torture. Captives can dramatically increase their endurance fitness by running on the spot or performing one-leg squats. Such physical exercise will significantly reduce stress levels and increase endurance conditioning should an escape attempt be made. These exercises will also increase the captive's amount and level of sleep, which will all add to his or her general well-being.

STAGE 5: DEPRESSION AND DESPAIR

This fifth stage can be much longer than previous stages and can last from weeks to months. Depression and severe apathy will inevitably set in after captives have been locked away for weeks and months in isolation, enduring repeated torture, beatings, general boredom, and lack of contact with the outside world.

Captives will have lost far more than just their freedom; almost everything else that they value—their family, their friends, and even their livelihood—are gone. Not only will they have lost contact with the world at large, their captors are likely to mislead them over the interest being shown by their government, employers, and family.

After victims have been held captive for so long, the indeterminate length of their stay in captivity will have severe mental repercussions. Depression will be exhibited by captives spending most of their time in bed and losing any appetite for the appalling food that they might have had. Depression and the concomitant severe weight loss will have a combined effect that could eventually lead to severe illness and possibly even death.

Depression, weight loss, and general apathy will inevitably lead to thoughts of suicide. These, however, are generally just depressive thoughts, and victims committing suicide while in captivity are rare to the point of being almost nonexistent.

Boredom is probably the most destructive element in this self-depreciating depression. Probably the most effective way of dealing with this, other than aggressive exercise, is for captives to utilize their intellect constructively. Even if just a single book is available to the captive, it can be read and reread, with new meanings found on each reading. Creative work, such as writing, drawing, or painting, can be extremely helpful. The humor of getting the better of the guards can be a great stress reliever and is something that can be enjoyed long after the event.

Even if paper, pens, and books are unavailable, captives can map out elaborate plans for the future, mentally design and furnish houses, and plan future holidays in the minutest detail. One captive,[2] deprived of paper and pencil, composed books of children's stories in his mind and after his release wrote and published the stories.

Virtually all captives will experience depression at some stage during their captivity. For some it is mild and fleeting, and for others it will be to the depths of being physically ill. The most common symptom of depression is gastrointestinal, but other symptoms may include dermatological, cardiovascular (hypertension), neurological (headache), and respiratory problems.

At this juncture, the captors have little to do with the captive other than to ensure that he or she remains in custody. Interrogation has probably run its course and ceased altogether, as there is little or no need for further statements to be released or video recordings to be made.

The guards will probably change several times to avert the consequential boredom they will inevitably be faced with, and it is at this stage that escape may become possible. The new guards will almost certainly have had little or nothing to do with the original kidnapping and have little interest in the boring routine they are obliged to maintain. It is this laxity that could provide opportunities for an escape attempt.

STAGE 6: GRADUAL ACCEPTANCE

The sixth stage can last from many months to years. Up until this point, the captive will have dismissed the idea that the incarceration will be projected, and it is at this juncture that it becomes abundantly clear that rescue or release is unlikely to occur in the near future.

This last stage of adjustment begins with the final realization that while waiting for rescue or release, captives must be more proactive in finding a use for their time if they are to successfully endure the ordeal of their incarceration.

The captive has to take the incarceration one day at a time and see what, if anything, it brings and not dwell on the future. Dwelling on the past can play its part in making the time go by, but little thought will generally be given to anything more than the following day. One obsession virtually all captives experience is what form the next meal will take, always hoping for something a little more edible. Days become structured by obsessive uniformity, with exercise periods, mealtimes, and bedtime becoming the highlights of the day.

People who were fastidious about their dress and personal appearance change into people with no social graces and a slovenly appearance, with bad language becoming the lingua franca. Interpersonal difficulties arise if there are other inmates, not from political or social standing but more from small-mindedness over personal habits.

Time passes in unrecognizable periods, with a day passing very slowly yet weeks and even months seemingly disappearing without notice. On release, captives have generally greatly miscalculated the time that has passed.

Initially, captives may, simply to pass the time, involve themselves in some creative project. But as time passes, the acquisition of new skills is tirelessly pursued, with the learning of a second language being the most common skill acquired. Other methods of coping with the boredom and incarceration include reading and writing. Letters are rarely delivered, but the writing of them gives the captive a great deal of self-satisfaction and a feeling of well-being. Even hard labor can become a coping strategy, as illustrated in Boulle's famous novel, *The Bridge over the River Kwai*.[3]

At this stage, normally the captors have given up the torture and beatings, and the need for video recordings has long passed. The sole purpose of the captors at this stage is custodial, ensuring that the captive stays alive and does not escape or attempt suicide. The captors are still hoping for a substantial ransom, and the captive's well-being, mental state, and appearance are all important at this juncture.

RELEASE

An oft-quoted statistic is that far more kidnap victims are killed during the rescue attempt than by their captors. Although this is largely true, it is the return to civilization that can be more traumatic than the captivity period itself. The transfer from brutality, isolation, near starvation, and a constant fear of execution to celebrity status, a clamoring press, and the concomitant sensory overload has led to suicide.

At this stage, the victim must be very careful, as the world's press will be outside the door, clamoring for interviews that must be studiously avoided until debriefing has finished. Information released at an inappropriate time could seriously affect not just the chances of survival of other hostages but also their chances of being rescued. It is also vitally important for identifying the captors, their modus operandi, their political or religious agenda, the safe houses and locations utilized, the weaponry they possess, and a hundred and one other vitally important pieces of information.

The first stage after release and debriefing should be an extensive period of care where the victim is afforded a complete medical, dental, psychiatric, and psychological assessment. This psychological assessment is carried out for a number of reasons but mainly to allow the debriefing team to assess the mental state of the victim. Once the victim's psychological state has been identified, the team can then identify the best line and mode of questioning.

The debriefing team is initially interested in what is called "perishable intelligence,"[4] and this will concern the presence of other hostages in the holding premises, their condition, and a detailed map of the premises for any subsequent rescue attempt. This "perishable information" concerns not any post-traumatic memory loss the victim might experience but rather information pertaining to other hostages, which might rapidly change as a result of information passed on during debriefing by the victim.

After this perishable intelligence has been obtained, there are, in the main, four additional areas of intelligence that the debriefing team will be seeking. These are generally considered to be security intelligence, law enforcement, general intelligence, and military intelligence.

Security intelligence: This will include details about the kidnapping itself, how and where it took place, the modus operandi of the group, the weapons used, the type and make of vehicles used, where any change of vehicles took place, any intermediate safe houses used, the final place of incarceration, the ethnicity of the captors, and so on. This will all assist in preventing future kidnappings and making any rescue attempts.

Law enforcement: That a crime has been committed is beyond doubt, but the information obtained from this part of the interview will assist in any future criminal prosecutions.

General intelligence: This covers everything that occurred while the victim was in captivity.

Military intelligence: For any future rescue attempt by Special Forces, the military will need to know as much as possible regarding the internal and external structure of the building. Even the minutest of details such as the positioning of light switches and security grills over windows; the location of tables, chairs, and beds; the direction in which doors open; and so on will be essential pieces of military intelligence. These data will be collated and examined to determine the best avenue of approach for a rescue attempt of others held in the same building.

The debriefing of details in relation to the actual method of kidnap will assist in identifying the gang or terrorists involved; their modus operandi; their preferred area of operations; the location of safe houses, cars, or vans used for transport; and most important the weaponry available. This will all require an extremely detailed level of recall from the victim. It may take some considerable period of time before all the relevant details can be extracted from the victim's memory because of the attendant post-traumatic stress.

This information could be critical to the survival and rescue of others who have been kidnapped, as well as for the security and the level of success for any future operations.

POST-TRAUMATIC STRESS

Post-traumatic stress can reveal itself under many guises, and even for experts in the field, it can be difficult to positively identify it as such. Some of the most common signals include the following:

- Insomnia
- Nightmares

- Flashbacks
- The shortening or lengthening of time
- Severe fatigue
- A lack of libido
- Social inhibitions
- Depression
- General anxiety
- Memory recall problems
- Fears of reprisal from the kidnappers
- Paranoia brought on by anything that resurrects memories of the victim's time in captivity

Any traumatic and stressful incident can trigger these reactions, and it is not an unusual mental complaint. The degree of post-traumatic stress is, as one would expect, dependent on many factors, not least of which is the individual's mental ability to cope with such stress and the level of the stress involved. For example, finding that your property has been burgled would be at one end of the stress scale, and spending years incarcerated, undergoing torture, beating, and mock executions would be at the other extreme end.

The symptoms can be reduced or even completely eliminated with physiotherapy and help from those experienced in the treatment of post-traumatic stress reactions. It is, however, vitally important that this treatment begin as soon as possible after the initial debriefing.

Critical incident stress management (CISM) is a widely debated way of coping with post-traumatic stress disorder.[5] CISM is a short-term psychological process that deals directly with the immediate stress. The method is concerned with mentally preparing potential victims with any stress problem that might arise because of the trauma, as well as post-stress trauma recovery. By identifying both ends of the problem, CISM attempts to return the victim to a normal life with only a limited degree of visible post-traumatic stress. Recent studies have, however, disputed the effectiveness of CISM,[6] and some studies have even reported that it may in fact exacerbate the problem to some degree.

AFTERMATH SURVIVAL

Managing to physically survive the incarceration and not be killed by the kidnappers is not the end of the battle. After release, victims should be forewarned by mental health professionals that they can expect feelings alternating between anger, sadness, and relief and even have thoughts of suicide.

There also may be long-range emotional reactions, such as depression or anxiety and sustained anger and bitterness toward the kidnappers. It is very important for victims of a kidnapping to be debriefed by a mental health professional and even have one on permanent call. It is also important that the victim realize that such feelings are normal after going through such a traumatic experience. Initial, and possibly longer term, counseling will enable the victim and his or her family to deal with these negative feelings in a positive way.

SOURCES

Judith Tebbutt, *A Long Walk Home: One Woman's Story of Kidnap, Hostage, Loss—and Survival* (Faber and Faber Non-Fiction, 2013).

Chris Ryan, *Alpha Force: Hostage: Book 3* (Red Fox, 2003).

R. H. Rahe, S. Karson, N. S. Howard, R. T. Rubin, and R. E. Poland, "Psychological and Physiological Assessments on American Hostages Freed from Captivity in Iran," *Psychosomatic Medicine* 52, no. 1 (1990): 1–16.

M. Schwinn and B. Diehl, *We Came to Help* (Harcourt, Brace, Jovanovich, 1976).

R. Stockdale and S. Stockdale, *In Love and War* (Harper and Row, 1984).

S. Wolf and H. S. Ripley, "Reactions among Allied Prisoners of War Subjected to Three Years of Imprisonment and Torture by the Japanese," *American Journal of Psychiatry* 104, no. 3 (1954): 180–93.

A. Guelke, "Hostage-Taking: A Renewed Tactic in Modern Conflict?" *Defense Analyst* 11, no. 3 (1995): 313–15.

D. R. McDuff, "Social Issues in the Management of Released Hostages," *Hospital and Community Psychiatry* 43, no. 8 (1992), 825–28.

R. H. Rahe and E. Genender, "Adaptation to and Recovery from Captivity Stress," *Military Medicine* 148, no. 7 (1983): 577–85.

Glenn R. Schiraldi, *The Post-Traumatic Stress Disorder Sourcebook: A Guide to Healing, Recovery, and Growth*, 2nd ed. (McGraw-Hill, 2009).

Mary Beth Williams, *The PTSD Workbook: Simple, Effective Techniques for Overcoming Traumatic Stress Symptoms*, 2nd ed. (New Harbinger Publications, 2013).

ENDNOTES

1. www.nato.int/docu/colloq/w970707/p6.pdf, and George Fink, ed., *Encyclopedia of Stress*, 3 vols. (Academic Press, 2000).

2. George Fink, ed., *Stress of War, Conflict and Disaster* (Academic Press, 2010).

3. Pierre Boulle, *The Bridge over the River Kwai*, reprint ed. (Presidio Press, 2007).

4. www.stratfor.com/.../20110927-above-tearline-intelligence-value-hostag...
5. wikipedia.org/wiki/Critical_incident_stress_management.
6. Bryan E. Bledsoe, "EMS Mythology, Part 3. EMS Myth #3: Critical Incident Stress Management (CISM) Is Effective in Managing EMS-Related Stress," *Emergency Medical Services* 32 no. 5 (2003): 77–80.

13

Hostage Negotiation

Although hostage negotiations do not really come within the purview of this book, the subject is included for the sake of completion. The following notes may, if read by high-risk victims, help them assess the situation in which they may find themselves and give them some idea as to how the kidnap negotiation process works and how long it is likely to take.

BASIC NEGOTIATION NOTES

During kidnap release and ransom negotiations, there are two potentially dangerous conditions that can occur: (1) confusion due to a lack of coordination between the kidnappers and the release team, resulting in misunderstandings, and (2) a badly planned and unsuccessful tactical assault. Poor tactical assaults by specialist forces always carry the highest mortality rate in a kidnap scenario. There are three main reasons for this:

1. The intervention by Special Forces would indicate that all reasonable attempts to resolve the kidnap situation by negotiation have failed.
2. Violence against the hostages is imminent or has already taken place.
3. A firefight ensues during which the victim is inadvertently injured or killed.

173

Kidnap incidents do vary greatly because of many factors; however, there are some basics that apply to all such kidnaps:

1. The kidnapper is carrying out the kidnap only to obtain something he desperately wants. It could be money, and often is, but it could also be to further the cause of his fanatical religious group, for some political leverage, or for the release of prisoners.
2. The kidnapper's objective is not the chosen victim but a third party who can fulfill the kidnapper's requirements.
3. The victim is simply someone who can be used by the kidnapper as an object to utilize in the bargaining process. The victim need not be affiliated with any political party, race, or religion and could be anyone chosen at random. Having said that, the higher the profile of the victim, the more likely it is that the kidnapper will be successful in satisfying all of his demands.

STAGES OF A KIDNAP SCENARIO

Kidnapping incidents generally progress through distinct stages.

Initial phase: This is often violent and short-lived. It will last just as long as it takes to subdue and secure the victim. Once the victim is at a secure location, this phase is at an end, and the kidnappers will begin to make their demands.

Negotiation: At this stage the police and/or military will be present, and the kidnappers' demands are under consideration. This part of the kidnap can last a matter of hours, but it will probably end up taking days or months. It is often referred to as "the standoff phase." This is generally a stagnant period, with neither the security personnel nor the kidnappers moving. It is during this phase that relationships have to be created between the kidnappers and hostages and the negotiators and kidnappers. During this period, the negotiator has to manipulate these relationships in a way that, hopefully, will lead to a successful outcome.

Termination phase: This is the final phase, which can be either violent or simply a peaceful handover of the victim. Basically there are three outcomes:

1. The kidnappers realize they are in a no-win situation, and they release the victim and are arrested.
2. Special Forces or sometimes the police antiterrorist team assault the building and kill or arrest the kidnappers.

3. The kidnappers' demands are acquiesced, and the kidnappers release the victims and are allowed to escape.

The final outcome as far as the hostages are concerned does not necessarily depend on what happens during stage three. If an assault is deemed necessary, then the victims may be accidentally killed by the assault team or deliberately killed by the kidnappers. Even if the kidnappers decide that they are in a no-win situation, they may kill the victims before surrendering. It may also be the case that the victims are killed during the negotiations. This is very common when terrorists, radical political groups, jihadists, or religious fanatics are involved.

Kidnappers have traded the lives of their kidnap victims for some political or religious gain to produce some of the most well-planned and successful kidnappings of recent times. These demands can be many and varied but usually involve the release of political prisoners, the payment of large sums of money to fund their cause, or simply a way to advertise their religious fanaticism.

Kidnapping can be considered to be a type of hostage situation. However, unlike a hostage situation where the hostage-takers are holed up in a known building, kidnappers keep their victims hidden away. Communication between the kidnappers and the negotiators is usually one-way, with the kidnappers making the demands. As a result, negotiations tend to be minimal.

Whatever the kidnappers' aims, the art of negotiating remains the same: to build an empathetic and close relationship with the kidnappers in an attempt to bring the situation to a successful and peaceful conclusion.

The first priority of a negotiator is to gather information about the victim and the condition he or she is in. Most of the local information will have been gleaned via the police, who will have run background checks on the kidnappers. The finite detail required by the negotiator can, however, be learned only by talking to the kidnappers themselves.

AIMS OF THE NEGOTIATOR

The first aim of the negotiator will be to discover the following:

- Who the kidnappers are
- How many victims are being held
- Whether the kidnappers are terrorists, jihadists, religious fanatics, or simple gang members

175

- What demands the kidnappers are making
- The name of the kidnappers' leader
- The number of kidnappers present

During this initial period, the negotiator will be paying close attention to the kidnapper's responses and general attitude. This will enable the negotiator to create a psychological profile of the kidnapper, his group, and their mental stability. With this psychological profile, the negotiator will be able to ascertain the kidnapper's response to different situations. If, for example, the kidnapper has suicidal tendencies, the negotiator will have to construct an approach that is completely different from one that deals with someone who is a jihadist or cold-blooded terrorist. The primary objectives of the negotiator in a kidnap situation are as follows.

Prolong the situation: The longer a kidnap situation lasts, the more likely that it will end peacefully. Tactics that can be utilized include the following:

- Waiting while someone with more authority is consulted
- Pushing back deadlines set by the kidnappers
- Getting the kidnappers bogged down in minutia such as what make and model of car they require or in what denomination they require the ransom
- Phrasing the question such that a lengthy answer is required rather than a simple yes or no

Ensure that the victim is safe: The negotiator must persuade the kidnappers to do the following:

- Release any victims who are sick or injured.
- Allow doctors or nurses to dispense medical treatment or drugs.
- Ensure that the victims have sufficient food and water.
- Try to negotiate for the release of as many victims as possible.

Reducing the number of victims being held not only ensures that they are safe but also simplifies the situation if an armed assault becomes necessary. In addition, any victims who are released will be able to supply important information regarding the kidnappers, their weapons, the condition of other victims, and the layout of the premises should an assault be undertaken.

Keep control and stay calm: From the very beginning through the initial hours of negotiation, the kidnappers can be extremely unstable,

176

and they will be high on adrenaline as a result of the kidnap. Unstable kidnappers wielding firearms could well be counterproductive to the victim's well-being.

At this juncture, arguing with the kidnappers will only exacerbate the situation. The negotiator should never refuse a demand made by the kidnappers but rather procrastinate or make a counteroffer. Whatever happens, the negotiator must remain positive and try to calm the kidnappers, reassuring them that the end result will be positive and result in a peaceful nonviolent resolution.

Encourage relationships between the negotiator, the kidnapper, and the victim: The negotiator must seem viable to the kidnapper by acting as if he or she is sympathetic with the kidnapper's aims and causes. This must be carried out in a way that doesn't demean the negotiator's stance and certainly not in a way that the negotiator seemingly supports the kidnapper's causes or religious fanaticism. Cooperation between the kidnapper and the victim such as the provision of food and medical supplies must be encouraged to form a basis of understanding and trust.

By encouraging the kidnappers to view the victim as a person rather than just a key to monetary or some other outcome will make it far more difficult for the kidnappers if they intend to execute him or her.

Illustrative Case

In a 1975 hostage standoff that occurred on a train in Holland, Robert de Groot,[1] who had been chosen for death, was reprieved after the terrorists heard him pray for his family's well-being. At this, some of the hostage-takers cried, and others agreed not to shoot him as they threw him off the moving train. Rolling down the embankment, he feigned death and escaped after the train had passed. After this the terrorists did not allow any prayers and had little compunction when shooting other hostages.

Make a deal: Successfully resolving a kidnap crisis necessitates the safe release of the victims and arrest of the kidnapper by the police. It is essential that the negotiator do everything in his or her power to ensure that the kidnappers trust and work with him or her to bring about a successful resolution and to save the victims' lives.

Attempting to intimidate or manipulate the kidnappers into ceding their demands will probably be counterproductive, especially if they are religious fanatics or terrorists, as this is counter to their whole ethos. Preserving the kidnappers' dignity is far more likely to result in a successful resolution than any other tactic.

Past experience has enabled a surrender protocol to evolve that can guide a negotiator to a safe and successful resolution of a kidnap situation. Protocols of this type, however, can be successful only if they are flexible, and each negotiator must be able to adapt the system to each and every kidnap situation. Each member of the team and any tactical units that are involved must understand the system adopted for a particular situation.

This will include details such as how the kidnappers will exit the scene, how the arrest will be performed and by whom, how the victims will be medically assessed, how the press will be briefed, how the victims will be transported to the debrief site, and so on. At this stage, it must be remembered that the protocol is not set in stone; it must be flexible and be discussable between the negotiator and the kidnapper until a mutually agreeable format is established.

During this negotiation period, words that should be avoided include *surrender, give up,* and anything else that confers the message that the kidnapper is about to lose face and be considered weak. The negotiator must utilize synonyms that will be more acceptable to the kidnapper such as *exit the building, abandon the fight,* and *allow the victim to be released,* as they will imply that the kidnapper is taking a positive self-elected decision to resolve the kidnap. It must be stressed what he has to gain by making the decision to come out at this particular time rather than wait and allow the crisis to deepen. The negotiator must emphasize the fact that realism coupled with optimism can reduce the damage so far caused and that nothing untoward has happened to this point in time. This will give the kidnapper an impression that he has a strong part to play in preventing the crisis from escalating further.

In the beginning, the kidnappers' demands will always be unreasonable, often demanding huge sums of money, the release of hundreds of prisoners, changes in legislation, a plane to escape in, and so on. Obviously, the negotiator can never submit to every demand, even if it would result in the safe release of the victims. National policies on kidnappers' demands, the availability of vast sums of money, the ability to release prisoners, and the requirement for discussions with political officials, the judiciary, and the military all limit what the negotiator can realistically offer the kidnappers. Governments have learned by hard lessons that giving in to such demands made by kidnappers and hostage-takers can only lead to a huge escalation in the number of such incidents. The negotiator can, however, ameliorate the deadlock over such demands by offering minor concessions, such as food, water, and medical supplies, together with promises of transportation and media coverage. In return, the kidnappers may be persuaded to release some of the victims, give up some of their weapons, or agree that their demands are excessive and downgrade them to more acceptable levels. By revisiting this process, the negotiator can slowly downgrade the kidnappers' position and demands.

Most countries do have official protocols and policies regarding the nonnegotiation with terrorists and other radicals; however, they do change. The policies also tend to be flexible depending on the "value" of the victim and whether children are involved. Even the most uncompromising of nonnegotiating governments can make exceptions. When such unreasonable demands are met, it is by way of secret deals that allow the government to save the hostages but still maintain its hard-line stance against terrorists.

Israel, Russia, the United Kingdom, France, and the United States all have a strict nonnegotiation policy. However, history has shown that every policy is open to exceptions. An example includes the TWA hijacking of Flight 847 by Hezbollah. Hezbollah sought the release of 700 Israeli prisoners who were Shiites. Although the hijackers killed one hostage, in total 766 Israeli prisoners were released in exchange for the surviving 138 passengers and 8 crew members.

While politically popular, a nonnegotiating policy with terrorists can often lead to tragic results. Negotiation can often be a means to a peaceful resolution even if a government or entity has no designs to give in to demands. The Beslan massacre in Russia in 2004 is an illustration of when the authorities refused to negotiate.[2] On the morning of September 1, over 30 armed Chechen separatists took over School Number 1 in Beslan, North Ossentia, in Russia. Among their demands was the withdrawal of Russian troops from Chechnya.

Specific numbers vary, but ultimately over 380 people died in total, over half of them schoolchildren. A number of hostages died as a direct result of the raid by authorities on the school. After three days of the standoff, the Chechen separatists—fully expecting they might die—had further entrenched themselves in their positions and were able to ensure the most amount of loss of life prior to their being overtaken. It is a sobering reminder that taking an extreme position in such delicate situations can have dire consequences.

SOURCES

Norman Antokol and Mayer Nudell, *No One a Neutral: Political Hostage-Taking in the Modern World* (Alpha Publications, 1990).

Clive C. Aston, *A Contemporary Crisis: Political Hostage-Taking and the Experience of Western Europe* (Greenwood Press, 1982).

Center for Contemporary Conflict, "The Moscow Hostage Crisis: An Analysis of Chechen Terrorist Goals," http://www.ccc.nps.navy.mil/si/may03/russia.asp.

Ralph Barker, *Not Here, but in Another Place* (St. Martin's, 1980).

BBC News, "1972: Olympic Hostages Killed in Gun Battle," http://news.bbc.co.uk/onthisday/hi/dates/stories/september/6/newsid_2500000/2500769.stm.

BBC News, "1976: Israelis Rescue Entebbe Hostages," http://news.bbc.co.uk/onthisday/hi/dates/stories/july/4/newsid_2786000/2786967.stm.

BBC News, "1977: Dutch Children Held Hostage," http://news.bbc.co.uk/onthisday/hi/dates/stories/may/23/newsid_2503000/2503933.stm.

Abraham Miller, *Terrorism and Hostage Negotiations* (Westview Press, 1980).

J. L. Greenstone, *The Elements of Police Hostage and Crisis Negotiations: Critical Incidents and How to Respond to Them* (Haworth Press, 2005).

F. J. Lanceley, *On-Scene Guide for Crisis Negotiators*, rev. ed. (CRC Press, 2003).

M. J. McMains and W. C. Mullins, *Crisis Negotiations: Managing Critical Incidents and Situations in Law Enforcement and Corrections*, rev. ed. (Anderson, 2006).

A. A. Slatkin, *Communication in Crisis and Hostage Negotiations* (Charles C Thomas, 2005).

T. Strentz, *Psychological Aspects of Crisis Negotiation* (CRC Press, 2006).

ENDNOTES

1. news.google.com/newspapers?nid=2519&dat=19751204.
2. http://philippineprisons.wordpress.com/2011/07/11/manual-of-hostage-negotiation/.

GLOSSARY

ACP: automatic Colt pistol—designation for ammunition originally designed for self-loading Colt pistols.

AP: armor-piercing bullet.

Armor-piercing bullet: bullet with a core made from tungsten or a tungsten alloy to assist in the penetration of armor plate.

Assault rifle: military firearm that is chambered for ammunition of reduced size, compared to a rifle round, and that has the capacity to switch between semiautomatic and fully automatic fire.

Ballistic inserts: name given to the rigid plates that are placed in front of soft body armor; their purpose is to break up high-velocity, hard-jacketed, and metal-penetrating missiles, allowing the underlying bullet-resistant material to capture the bullet.

Ballistics nylon: a copolymer of the basic polyamide used in WWII against shrapnel from munitions but of little use against bullets other than low-velocity soft-lead projectiles.

Bird shot: usually refers to No. 6 shot, which is used for shooting birds and small game; this shot is 0.36″ (9.1 mm) in diameter.

Bride kidnapping: a practice throughout history and around the world in which a man abducts the woman he wishes to marry.

BRV: bullet-resistant vest.

Bullet: a nonspherical missile for use in rifled barrels.

Bullet, full metal jacket (FMJ): bullet which has a lead core covered with a hard metal jacket, leaving only the base exposed. The jacket can be of almost any material, although brass and steel are the most common. It is also referred to as *full metal case, fully jacketed,* and *ball ammunition.*

Bullet, hollow point: bullet with a cavity in the nose to assist in expansion when it strikes tissue; often wrongly referred to as a Dum-Dum bullet.

Bullet jacket: metal covering of a jacketed bullet.

Cartridge: an imprecise term usually referring to a single, live, unfired round of ammunition composed of a missile, cartridge case, propellant, and primer; the correct term is, a *round* of ammunition.

Cell phone: also referred to as a mobile phone.

CS: 2-chlorobenzalmalononitrile, a man-made chemical used in tear gas sprays; commonly used by the police, military, and security personnel.

Defensive driving: driving techniques to reduce your chance of being kidnapped from your car.

Dilatant liquid: another name for a sheer thickening liquid.

Disconnecter: trigger disconnecter is a type of safety in a firearm that prevents the trigger from being held down after a shot has been fired. This disallows either automatic fire or deliberate "slamfire," depending on the particular firearm's action.

Double action: weapon which has a long, relatively heavy pull on the trigger that cocks then drops the hammer all in one action.

Dum-Dum bullet: soft point .303″ caliber rifle bullets made by the Dum-Dum armory in India. Hollow point bullets are often wrongly called Dum-Dum bullets.

Dust shot: very small lead balls used in shotgun ammunition. The diameter is usually 0.08″ (2.0 mm).

Express kidnapping: kidnap victims are temporarily detained and forced to withdraw large sums of money from cash points (ATMs).

FMJ: full metal jacketed bullet.

Fore end: a wood or plastic piece that is usually designed with a semi-circular groove to fit under the barrel of a gun and is attached by metal fastening devices; it is shaped to fit the hand and is used to steady the weapon during firing or to operate the feed mechanism in a pump action shotgun.

Hammerless firearm: firearm in which the hammer is situated within the weapon's frame or one in which the firing pin is spring-loaded and does not require a hammer.

Hard plate insert: steel, titanium alloy, or heat-treated aluminum plates placed in pockets on the front and rear of a BRV to increase its effectiveness.

Hollow point (HP): bullet with a cavity in the nose to aid its expansion when hitting the target.

HOSDB: United Kingdom's Home Office Scientific Development Branch.

Jacketed bullet: bullet with a lead core covered in a copper/zinc alloy.

Kevlar: aramid fiber used in BRVs and fabric-based tires.

Mobile phone: also referred to as a cell phone.

NIJ: U.S. National Institute of Justice.

OC: oleo capsicum, a natural ingredient obtained from chilies and used in tear gas sprays.

Opaque armor: opaque armor can be made of many different materials, including tempered steel, ballistic nylon, synthetic fibers (Kevlar, Spectra, etc.), and other composite materials. Most of the synthetic materials are lighter than steel but stronger in certain applications.

Pistol: basically a handgun. In English terminology, a weapon can be a self-loading pistol, a revolving pistol, or a single-shot pistol. In American terminology, a pistol is generally either a self-loading pistol or a single-shot pistol.

Push dagger: small dagger designed to be held in the fist and delivered with a punch. It is made by Cold Steel and other manufacturers.

Revolver: handgun that has a series of chambers in a cylinder mounted in line with the barrel. A mechanism revolves the cylinder so the chambers are successively aligned with the bore. Only the chamber that is, at any one time, in line with the bore is fired.

RN: round-nosed bullet configuration.

Self-loading pistol: a repeating firearm requiring a separate pull of the trigger for each shot fired. After the first round from the magazine is manually loaded, the weapon will use the energy of discharge to eject the fired cartridge and load a new cartridge from the magazine into the barrel, ready for firing. In American nomenclature, it can also be referred to as an *auto* or a *pistol*.

Shear thickening liquid: a liquid that solidifies on impact.

Shot: spherical pellets, generally of lead, loaded into shotgun cartridges.

Shotgun 12 bore: shotgun barrel in which a perfectly fitting round ball weighs one-twelfth of a pound. The internal diameter of a 12 bore weapon is 0.729".

Shotgun pump action: a type of breech closure that is accomplished through an operating rod attached to a moveable fore end. This fore end is moved back and forward to open and close the action. It is also called *slide action.*

Single action: weapon in which a hammer that must be manually cocked; a short, relatively light pull on the trigger will then fire the weapon.

Slamfire: a pump action weapon, where the gun fires immediately, the weapon's action is cycled, and the bolt closes on a fresh round.

Small arms: generally any weapons less than .50" caliber.

Spalling: a mechanism in bullet-resistant glass caused by the glass bulging away from the strike face of the glass sheet, throwing shards of glass off the opposite side.

Spectra: high molecular weight polyethylene fabric used in BRVs.

SRV: stab-resistant vest.

Stun gun: an electrical self-defense device that uses high voltage to stop an attacker.

Surveillants: those who conduct surveillance.

Tear gas: a nonlethal chemical designed to produce severe burning to the eyes and skin.

Windmill effect: involves a victim swinging the arms wildly to make it difficult for an abductor to maintain a hold on him or her.

APPENDIX I: TERRORIST GROUPS THAT MAY BE INVOLVED IN KIDNAPPING

The various terrorist groups that may be linked to kidnapping and the countries they operate in are listed in the following table.

Organization	AUS	CAN	FRA	UK	IND	RUS	PRC	TUR	TUN	IRN
Abdullah Azzam Shaheed Brigade					X					
Abu Nidal Organization		X	X	X	X					
Abu Sayyaf	X	X		X	X					
Aden-Abyan Islamic Army		X		X						
Akhil Bharat Nepali Ekta Samaj						X				
al-Aqsa Foundation			X							
al-Aqsa Martyrs Brigades		X	X		X					
Al-Badr						X				
al-Gama'aal-Islamiyya		X	X	X	X		X			
Al Ghurabaa				X						
al-Haramain Foundation							X			
Al-Itihaadal-Islamiya		X		X						
al-Qaeda	X	X	X	X	X	X	X			
al-Qaeda in Iraq	X	X		X	X					
al-Qaeda in the Arabian Peninsula	X	X			X					
al-Qaeda in the Islamic Maghreb	X	X			X		X			
Al-Shabaab	X	X		X	X					
Al-Umar-Mujahideen						X				
All Tripura Tiger Force						X				
Ansar al-Islam	X	X		X	X					
Ansar al-Sharia (Tunisia)										X
Ansar Dine					X					
Ansaru				X						
Armed Islamic Group of Algeria		X		X						

Organization								
Army of Islam					X			X
Aum Shinrikyo					X			X
Babbar Khalsa							X	X
Babbar Khalsa International						X	X	X
Balochistan Liberation Army						X		
Caucasus Emirate			X		X			
Central Intelligence Agency								
Communist Party of India (Maoist)				X				
Communist Party of India (Marxist–Leninist)				X				
Communist Party of the Philippines/New People's Army					X		X	
Communist Party of Turkey/Marxist–Leninist	X							
Conspiracy of Fire Nuclei					X			
Continuity Irish Republican Army					X	X		
Cumann na mBan						X		
Deendar Anjuman				X				
Dukhtaran-e-Millat				X				
East Turkestan Information Center		X						
East Turkestan Islamic Movement		X			X			
East Turkestan Liberation Organization		X						
Egyptian Islamic Jihad			X					X

Continued

189

Organization	AUS	CAN	FRA	UK	IND	RUS	PRC	TUR	TUN	IRN
El Kaide Terör Örgütü Türkiye Yapılanması									X	
ETA		X		X	X					
Fianna Éireann				X						
Great Eastern Islamic Raiders' Front			X						X	
Hamas		X	X		X					
Haqqani Network					X					
Harkat-ul-Jihad al-Islami				X	X					
Harkat-ul-Jihad al-Islami in Bangladesh				X	X					
Harkat-ul-Mujahideen		X		X	X					
Harakat-ul-Mujahideen/Alami				X		X				
Hezb-e-Islami Gulbuddin		X		X						
Hezbollah		X		X	X				X	
Hezbollah External Security Organisation	X	X		X						
Hezbollah Military Wing			X	X						
Hilafet Devleti									X	
Hizbul Mujahideen			X			X				
Hizbut-Tahrir							X			
Hofstad Network			X							
Holy Land Foundation for Relief and Development			X		X					
Indian Mujahideen					X	X				

Organisation						
International Sikh Youth Federation			X		X	
Irish National Liberation Army			X			X
Irish People's Liberation Organisation			X	X		
Islamic Jihad–Jamaat Mujahideen	X					X
Islamic Jihad Movement in Palestine		X	X	X		
Islamic Jihad Union			X	X		
Islamic Movement of Uzbekistan	X		X	X		X
Izz ad-Din al-Qassam Brigades	X	X		X		
Jabhatal-Nusra	X		X			
Jaish-e-Mohammed	X		X	X	X	
Jamaah Ansharut Tauhid			X		X	
Jamaat Ansar al-Sunna			X			
Jamaat ul-Furquan			X			
Jamaat-ul-Mujahideen Bangladesh			X	X		
Jamiat al-Islah al-Idzhtimai						X
Jamiat-e Islami	X					
Jamiat-ul-Ansar	X		X			X
Jemaah Islamiyah			X	X		X
Jundal-Sham						
Jundallah				X		
Kach and Kahane Chai	X		X	X		
Kanglei Yawol Kanna Lup				X		
Kangleipak Communist Party				X		
Kata'ib Hezbollah		X				

Continued

191

Organization	AUS	CAN	FRA	UK	IND	RUS	PRC	TUR	TUN	IRN
Khalistan Commando Force						X				
Khalistan Zindabad Force			X			X				
Khuddamul-Islam				X					X	
Kurdistan Democratic Party–North			X							
Kurdistan Freedom Falcons			X	X					X	
Kurdistan Workers' Party	X	X	X	X	X					
Lashkar-e-Jhangvi	X	X		X	X					
Lashkar-e-Taiba	X	X		X	X	X	X			
Liberation Tigers of Tamil Eelam	X	X	X	X	X	X				
Libyan Islamic Fighting Group				X	X					
Loyalist Volunteer Force				X						
Manipur People's Liberation Front						X				
Maoist Communist Centre of India						X			X	
Marxist–Leninist Communist Party									X	
Moroccan Islamic Combatant Group				X	X					
Muslim Brotherhood							X			
National Democratic Front of Bodoland						X				
National Liberation Army		X	X		X					
National Liberation Front of Tripura						X				
Orange Volunteers				X						
Osbat al-Ansar		X		X	X		X			
Palestine Liberation Front		X			X					
People's Congress of Ichkeria and Dagestan							X			

192

People's Liberation Army of Manipur		X				
People's Revolutionary Party of Kangleipak		X				
Popular Front for the Liberation of Palestine			X		X	X
Popular Front for the Liberation of Palestine–General Command			X		X	X
Provisional Irish Republican Army				X		
Real Irish Republican Army				X	X	
Red Hand Commando				X	X	
Red Hand Defenders			X	X		
Revolutionary Armed Forces of Colombia			X	X	X	X
Revolutionary Organization of the 17th November			X	X	X	
Revolutionary Party of Kurdistan	X					
Revolutionary People's Liberation Party–Front	X		X	X	X	X
Revolutionary Struggle			X			
Saor Éire						
Tevhid-Selam (Kudüs Ordusu)	X					
The Saved Sect					X	
Shining Path			X		X	X
Sipah-e-Sahaba Pakistan						X

Continued

Organization	AUS	CAN	FRA	UK	IND	RUS	PRC	TUR	TUN	IRN
Society of the Revival of Islamic Heritage							X			
Stichting Al Aqsa			X							
Students Islamic Movement of India						X				
Supreme Military Majlis ul-Shura of the United Mujahideen Forces of Caucasus							X			
Takfir wal-Hijra			X							
Taliban							X			
Tehreek-e-Nafaz-e-Shariat-e-Mohammadi				X						
Tehrik-i-Taliban Pakistan		X			X					
Tamil Nadu Liberation Army						X				
Tamil National Retrieval Troops						X				
Ulster Defence Association				X						
Ulster Volunteer Force				X						
United Liberation Front of Assam						X				
United National Liberation Front						X				
United Self-Defense Forces of Colombia		X			X					
Vanguards of Conquest		X								
World Tamil Movement		X								
World Uygur Youth Congress								X		

Note: AUS = Australia, CAN = Canada, FRA = France, UK = United Kingdom, IND = India, RUS = Russia, PRC = Peoples Republic of China, TUR = Turkey, TUN = Tunisia, IRN = Iran.

APPENDIX 2: GENERAL CONVERSION VALUES

To Convert From	To	Multiply By
Feet/sec	Meters/sec	0.0508
Feet/sec	Miles/hour	0.6818
Foot pounds	Ergs	1.35582×10^7
Foot pounds	Joules	1.35582
Foot pounds	Kg meters	0.138255
Gravitational constant	Cm (sec × sec)	980.621
Gravitational constant	Ft (sec × sec)	32.1725
Joules (Int)	Foot pounds	0.737684
Joules (Int)	Foot poundals	23.73428
Meters/sec	Ft/min	196.85039
Meters/sec	Ft/sec	3.2808399
Length		
Centimeters	Feet	0.0328
Centimeters	Inches	0.3937
Decimeters	Inches	3.937
Feet	Centimeters	30.48
Feet	Decimeters	3.048
Feet	Meters	0.3048
Inches	Centimeters	2.54
Inches	Millimeters	25.4
Kilometers	Feet	3280.8
Kilometers	Meters	1000
Kilometers	Miles	0.62137
Kilometers	Yards	1093.6
Meters	Inches	39.3701
Meters	Kilometers	0.001
Meters	Miles, statute	0.000621
Meters	Millimeters	1000

Continued

To Convert From	To	Multiply By
Meters	Millimicrons	1×10^9
Micron	Centimeters	0.0001
Micron	Inches	3.9370079×10^{-5}
Miles	Kilometers	1.6093
Miles	Meters	1609.3
Millimeters	Inches	0.03937
Yards	Centimeters	91.44
Yards	Meters	0.9144
Weight		
Grams	Grains	15.432
Grams	Kilograms	0.001
Grams	Micrograms	1×10^6
Grams	Milligrams	1000
Grams	Ounces (avoirdupois)	0.03527
Grams	Pounds (avoirdupois)	0.002205
Pounds (avoirdupois)	Grains	7000
Pounds (avoirdupois)	Grams	453.59
Pounds (avoirdupois)	Kilograms	0.4536
Pounds (avoirdupois)	Ounces (avoirdupois)	16

APPENDIX 3: BRITISH HOME OFFICE STANDARDS FOR BULLET- AND STAB-RESISTANT VESTS

HOSDB (2007) Ballistic Standard: Handgun

Level	Ammunition	Bullet Mass (g)	Velocity (m/s)	Max Trauma (mm)
HG1/A	9 mm FMJ (DM11A1B2)	8.0	355–375	44
	.357 Mag JSP (Rem R357M3)	10.2	380–400	
HG1	9 mm FMJ (DM11A1B2)	8.0	355–375	25
	.357 Mag JSP (Rem R357M3)	10.2	380–400	
HG2	9 mm FMJ (DM11A1B2)	8.0	420–440	25
	.357 Mag JSP (Rem R357M3)	10.2	445–465	
HG3	5.56 × 45 mm SP (LE223T3)	4.0	735–765	25

HOSDB (2007) Ballistic Standard: Rifle and Shotgun

Level	Ammunition	Bullet Mass (g)	Velocity (m/s)	Max Trauma (mm)
RF1	7.62 × 51 mm FMJ Ball (L2A2)	9.3	815–845	25
RF2	7.62 × 51 mm FMJ AP (L40A1)	9.7	835–865	25
SG1	12 ga Winchester 1 oz slug	28.4	410–460	25

HOSDB (2007) Knife and Spike Standard

Level	Energy Level E1 (Joules)		Penetration (mm) Knife Spike		Energy Level E2 (Joules)	Penetration (mm) Knife Spike	
KR1	24	7	—		36	20	—
KR1 + SP1	24	7	0		36	20	—
KR2	33	7	—		50	20	—
KR2 + SP2	33	7	0		50	20	—
KR3	43	7	—		65	20	—
KR3 + SP3	43	7	0		65	20	—

APPENDIX 4: NATIONAL INSTITUTE OF JUSTICE STANDARDS FOR BULLET-RESISTANT VESTS

Armor Level Protection	
Type I (.22 LR, .380 ACP)	.22 long rifle lead round-nose (LR LRN) bullets at a velocity of 329 m/s (1,080 ft/s ± 30 ft/s) 6.2 g (95 gr) .380 ACP full metal jacketed round-nose (FMJ RN) bullets at a velocity of 322 m/s (1,055 ft/s ± 30 ft/s) It is no longer part of the standard.
Type IIA (9 mm, .40 S&W, .45 ACP)	9 × 19 mm parabellum FMJ RN bullets at a velocity of 373 m/s (1,225 ft/s) 11.7 g (180 gr) .40 S&W full metal jacketed (FMJ) bullets at a velocity of 352 m/s (1,155 ft/s) .45 ACP FMJ bullets at a velocity of 275 m/s (900 ft/s)
Type II (9 mm, .357 Magnum)	9 mm FMJ RN bullets at a velocity of 398 m/s (1,305 ft/s) .357 Magnum jacketed soft point bullets at a velocity of 436 m/s (1,430 ft/s)
Type IIIA (.357 SIG, .44 Magnum)	.357 SIG FMJ flat-nose (FN) bullets at a velocity of 448 m/s (1,470 ft/s) .44 Magnum semijacketed hollow point bullets at a velocity of 436 m/s (1,430 ft/s)
Type III (rifles)	7.62 × 51 mm NATO M80 ball bullets at a velocity of 847 m/s (2,780 ft/s) It also provides protection against the threats mentioned in Types I, IIA, II, and IIIA.
Type IV (armor-piercing rifle)	.30-06 Springfield M2 armor-piercing (AP) bullets at a velocity of 878 m/s (2,880 ft/s) It also provides at least single-hit protection against the threats mentioned in Types I, IIA, II, IIIA, and III.

APPENDIX 5: NATIONAL INSTITUTE OF JUSTICE STANDARD 0115.00 FOR STAB-RESISTANT BODY ARMOR

NIJ Standard: 0115.00 Stab Resistance of Personal Body Armor

Protection Level	"E1" Strike Energy		"E2" Overtest Strike Energy	
	J	ft. lbf	J	ft. lbf
1	24 ± 0.50	17.7 ± 0.36	36 ± 0.60	26.6 ± 0.44
2	33 ± 0.60	24.3 ± 0.44	50 ± 0.70	36.9 ± 0.51
3	43 ± 0.60	31.7 ± 0.44	65 ± 0.80	47.9 ± 0.59

APPENDIX 6: COMMERCIAL AND GENERAL ABBREVIATIONS FOR BULLET CONFIGURATIONS

Abbreviation	Bullet Type
ACP	Automatic Colt pistol. This is used as a designation for cartridges designed specifically for self-loading pistol cartridges (i.e., .380 ACP, .45 ACP). It can also be in lowercase (i.e., .380 acp or .45 acp).
AP	Armor-piercing bullet. It usually has a tungsten core.
FMJ	Full metal jacket. This is a jacketed bullet with lead core exposed at the base.
JHP	Jacketed hollow point. Jacketed bullets have a hole in the tip to promote expansion on impact.
LRN	Lead round nose.
Mag.	Magnum. This specifies cartridges of a higher power of that standard (i.e., .41 Rem Mag., .44 Mag.).
+P	"Plus P" (10 percent to 15 percent over pressure). This is a high-pressure cartridge for use in standard weapons where greater power is required.
+P+	"Plus P Plus" (20 percent to 25 percent over pressure). This is the same as with +P but even more powerful. This is recommended for weapons only with a strong steel frame and usually sold only to law enforcement agencies.
PB	Parabellum. This includes 9 × 19 mm and 7.65 × 19 mm cartridges with the Latin designation parabellum (i.e., for war).
RN	Round nose. There is an ogival nose shape to the bullet.
RNL	Round-nosed lead. This is a plain lead bullet with an ogive-shaped nose.

Continued

203

Abbreviation	Bullet Type
S&W	Smith and Wesson. This designation is used for cartridges designed specifically for Smith and Wesson–designed weapons (i.e., .38 S&W revolver).
SMP	Semipointed bullet.
SP	Soft point. This is a jacketed bullet with an exposed lead tip.
WC	Wadcutter. This is essentially a round-nosed bullet without the round nose. It gives a sharp edge for cutting clean holes in the target when target shooting.

INDEX